Insight On Trumpism And The Only Thing That Can Save USA From Total Doom

CURRENT EVENT, CHRISTIAN LADY IN JAIL:
Sure, the USA is a nation ruled by law instead of man; I for one believe the law must be upheld under all conditions and at all cost, period. Catalyst, catalyst, catalyst, there is something called human nature, and right now in the great USA moral decay and culture rot is a bigger threat to USA survival than even economic doom in this writer's view.

Repeal the arch-evil 1938 socialist minimum wage law and let a real true free market place economy save this great nation before it is too late. I double dog dare the USA to act now while we still have a chance to save a hundred million or more lives.

Be aware, this writer believes this Christian lady in jail has the potential to light a huge gay backlash fuse if she is not somehow freed from jail, the overly severe punishment is creating a Christian Martyr. That is just this writer's opinion.

Now a few words about the Trump effect: What I like about Trump is he is a man of action and I would vote for him in a New York minute. This drip, drip, by drip with everyone standing around watching liberalism bury this great nation alive I feel is the worst possible way to go out.

The real skinny on this is my personal view is Trump can't save the USA, in fact no individual or movement can. The only thing that can possibly save the USA at this late liberalism engulfed stage is a real pure free market place economy. And all it will take to get a real pure free market place economy is to repeal the 1938 minimum wage law, period. Duh.
SIRMANS LOG: 06 SEPTEMBER 2015, 0816 HOURS.

Insight On Trumpism And The Only Thing That Can Save USA From Total Doom

WILL USA SURVIVE COMING COLLAPSE VERSUS BACK TO THE STONE AGE

As a great creative writer with almost supernatural wisdom so many times I have felt that my writing is totally ignored. But, deep down I know that can't possibly be true. Sure, after nearly eighty years as a welfare state for the most part in the USA sound judgment accompanying a strong survival instinct may be in question.

I have no way of proving it but I believe around the world some may see my writing as the gospel truth. Also, I believe around the world some may see the USA as like an injured wild beast, which is the most dangerous thing there is.

Despite all of the USA culture, moral, and economic problems without a doubt everyone around the world knows even with a declining image this North American giant is still the most powerful military and economic force on earth. A free nation demands from its citizen's responsibility and accountability, otherwise at some point the iron fist will not be denied.

In my view it is a given the USA economy will soon collapse no matter what action is taken, and I pray that I'm wrong on this. My grave concern and purpose is to help save as many as possible through the collapse and past it. And to do that the must thing is to get the government as much as possible and as soon as possible out of the family provider business.

It is critical that we get as many people as possible back to depending on themselves and their fellow man as soon as possibly. The fact is very simple when the full collapse hit the USA government won't have the

Insight On Trumpism And The Only Thing That Can Save USA From Total Doom

means to take care of anyone and will be lucky to be able to maintain order.

When I plead and I cry to repeal the arch-evil 1938 socialist minimum wage law, that law in itself has no power, but it is the key that will unlock and free up a real true free market place economy. And a real true free market place economy is one of the most powerful things on earth.

It will give back power and survivability control to the people so when the collapse hit and government can't provide, the people can survive on their own. Nothing is going to stop this coming collapse, but a real true free market place economy is the only thing that can give the USA a fighting chance to survive through it.

Otherwise, for the great USA it may mean back to the Stone Age. Failure to heed my great almost supernatural wisdom advice on this is beyond my power or control, so let the record stand, I did my duty, so be it.

SIRMANS LOG: 02 SEPTEMBER 2015, 1951 HOURS.

ADD ON #1

Sure, before the arch-evil 1938 socialist minimum wage law the USA had many problems, but culture rot and moral decay was not one of them as it is today. Before 1938 the USA had a real true free market place economy minus our evil liberal enacted socialist law giving government the power to set wages and prices over all private businesses in the USA.

In one swoop that arch-evil socialist law destroyed the right of the private business sector to control its on destiny by being able to set its own wages and prices.

Insight On Trumpism And The Only Thing That Can Save USA From Total Doom

By losing that right and power the USA economy lost its disciplining power to purge thereby leaving the economy with no way to weed out waste and inefficiency, including liberalism.

What we have today, as an economy in the USA is a phony weak pretender that is powerless to defend and protect itself or the nation's culture, moral, and spiritual values. Without repealing this evil law quickly the USA will soon be left with millions upon millions of helpless dependents that will die due to a collapsed penniless USA government.

I dare you, prove my prediction wrong. God help us.
SIRMANS LOG: 03 SEPTEMBER 2015, 1617 HOURS.

ADD ON #2
The economic boom and bust cycle is part of nature just like the life and death cycle. No matter how good the medical care sooner or later the grim reaper won't be put off any longer. The time is up and the collapse (bust cycle) won't be put off much longer.

Our human responsibility is to be prepared to survive through the cycles and it can't be done without a strong nuclear and extended family system. No society or civilization has ever survived without a strong nuclear and extended family system, period. And right now the USA nuclear and extended family system is in almost total ruins.

Repealing the 1938 minimum wage law will restore the USA nuclear and extended family system but the problem is there is so little time left before this collapse hit. Lord help us.

Insight On Trumpism And The Only Thing That Can Save USA From Total Doom

SIRMANS LOG: 04 SEPTEMBER 2015, 0957 HOURS.

ADD ON#3
Another thing I've decided to comment on is this shallow minded liberal technique of trying to entrap people by asking gotcha questions. Sure, most everyone knows that being informed is very important when running for political office. But, do the shallow minded liberal asking that type of question truly understand why there is a need to have libraries, I doubt it.

Only a fool is willing to clutter his/her mind with all kinds of needless details. In terms of leadership it is far more important to have the ability to know where and how to find what one needs to know than to try micromanaging things.

I think the best thing is to just say up front, I'll answer your questions but I'm not here to take a quiz, then stand your ground because going down that road places one in a no win situation.

SIRMANS LOG: 04 SEPTEMBER 2015, 1518 HOURS.

USA: TO ACT, OR NOT TO ACT AND DIE.
Talk, talk, talk, liberalism and the welfare state it have created continue to nail the lid on the USA coffin. The older I get the more I am convinced that by and large people are going to do what they can get away with. All of this culture rot and moral decay liberalism has brought upon this great nation will never be cleaned-up with just talk, talk, talk.

It all starts with how we raise our young, period. These perpetrators that are committing all of these horrendous crimes was never conditioned to fear

Insight On Trumpism And The Only Thing That Can Save USA From Total Doom

punishment for wrongdoing when being raised. The more one has to earn and struggle for life the more precious and valuable life becomes. That is a fact and there is no way around it, yet liberalism totally disregards and ignores this fact.

These perpetrators has never been conditioned to respect other people's feelings and property, all they know is me first, I want mine, I want it all and any consequences is the furthest thing from there mind. So, until liberalism is bridled and brought under control the great USA will soon be history. And I will bet the farm on that. Action is what it is going to take to save this great USA the land of almost unlimited individual freedom.

One way or another we as a nation must act and get the ball rolling no matter right or wrong. Repealing the arch-evil 1938 socialist minimum wage law will definitely get the ball rolling no matter right or wrong because the worst thing is not to act at all.

If the action is proven wrong the nation will be forced to correct that wrong because any action is better than to do nothing but talk, talk, talk. It is not about this writer being right or wrong it is about the survival of my beloved homeland, period.

SIRMANS LOG: 01 SEPTEMBER 2015, 0017 HOURS.

PS: TAKE HEED: AN OLD BIBLICAL TRUTH, "Blessed are the meek, for they will inherit the earth". Writer's injection: Remember it said the meek would inherit the earth not the weak, like the now predominant liberalism victimized USA has become.

Insight On Trumpism And The Only Thing That Can Save USA From Total Doom

In fact I believe that is one of the reasons Trump is so popular he stands up to liberalism and faces it down. In my view liberalism is an aggressive destructive form of existence and is just like all threatening intimidating boogie man type facades.

All one has to do is stand your ground and face it down and it will retreat as just pesky noise with no bite.

GUNS VERSUS A FREE USA!

Myself, I am nonviolent and believe in nonviolence except in cases of self-defense and personal protection. However, I thank God for the USA's second amendment and this nation's citizens right to bear arms.

I believe freedom and the citizen's right to bear arms goes hand in hand. And if you take away the citizen's right to bear arms it won't be long before government nips individual freedom in the bud. Sure, the USA may have more gun deaths than any other nation but it also has far more individual freedom than any other nation, and that is why so many is trying to get here.

The core USA violence problem is not the gun, The gun has not all but totally destroyed our culture, moral and spiritual values, or left us with a phony weak p.... of an economy. No, it is liberalism riding shotgun with its created welfare state that has brought the great USA to its knees, and will finish us off unless the arch evil 1938 socialist minimum wage law is repealed.

Many years ago in rural areas and small towns guns were everywhere and a multiple killings was something almost unheard of. Back then most people never even bothered to lock their doors at night or anytime, so,

Insight On Trumpism And The Only Thing That Can Save USA From Total Doom

what has changed, liberalism. Because back then about the only place you could fine a liberal was in a rich family or maybe on a collage campus, and almost never was a liberal to be found among the poor.

Bam! Then came the "New deal" fortified with the arch evil 1938 minimum wage law and since then liberalism has never looked back and to this day is about to drive the final nail into our coffin. Today practical the entire poor is liberal with an entitlement mentality and killing more future unborn babies in the womb than any other group, God help us. In my one man opinion I believe the real culprit is liberalism and its created welfare state, period.

Liberalism has corrupted so many people judgment that few can recognize a moral threat or have the wisdom to know what real compassion is. Almost everyone today is doting on their children and spoiling there pets while letting strong discipline and self-sacrifice teaching go by the way side. Our children are 100 percent of the nations future and how we raise them is everything if the nation is to survive.

How can you expect someone to be responsible and accountable with self-restraint when they have never been raised and conditioned to be that way, you can't. I for one think medical supervised flogging ought to be considered for young law-breakers, but that type of thinking today is seen as extremely cruel and uncivilized.

Sure, it will cause some sore Asses and hurt feelings but it wouldn't kill anyone. It would save ten times more of our ill raised youngsters than our correction systems is saving today and wouldn't have to house and feed anyone. Yet, compassion like everything else

Insight On Trumpism And The Only Thing That Can Save USA From Total Doom

today is upside down. Especially the poor and so many others are just not raising our young to be law abiding and productive future citizens today.

When nuts with a gun go shooting and killing up people it is because they are so self-centered that they hardly know what a self-sacrifice is and has never been conditioned with self-restraint when young on how to deal with personal frustrations, period.

There is more than one way to skin a cat, and I'll admit that my cold hard tough love may be too much, but we are losing this great country and rescuing the young is a must, this writer just can't look the other way. Again, I say get the ball rolling by repealing the 1938 minimum wage law now that is the USA only chance of coming out of this fix alive. I ask in your name, God save this great land of individual freedom. **SIRMANS LOG: 27 AUGUST 2015, 1350 HOURS.**

ADD ON #1
More about the Trump effect: Demographics, demographics, demographics, that and scientific polling is what the establishment and political promoters lives on. I for one believe depending on that only will never enable them to ever understand the Trump effect.

Everyone knows the establishment and others are waiting and hoping for the Trump movement to self-destruct or peter out, and the sooner the better. I believe because of human nature they may be in for an awful long wait.

Sure, with modern scientific polling pandering to demographic groups has become an art that the so-

Insight On Trumpism And The Only Thing That Can Save USA From Total Doom

called political experts have used very successful in the past, but it is not an advantage against Trump.

There are some demographics percentages that are not going to vote republican under any circumstance and on the other hand some demographics percentages are not going to vote democratic under any circumstance. However, at heart we all know right from wrong whether we admit or not. And we all know Trump is definitely telling the truth with the things he is saying.

So, I will wrap this up by saying: Trump is going over the heads of demographics and appealing directly to truth, decently, and the people's self-interest. And that is something that can't be dismissed as just a passing fad.
So, the people are only choosing realness, truth, decency, and self-interest over fake, pandering, selling out, etc.

Liberalism has brought this great nation to this sad state, repealing the 1938 minimum wage law is the only thing that can bridle liberalism and bring back some sanity to this nation, period.
SIRMANS LOG: 28 AUGUST 2015, 1432 HOURS.

ADD ON #2
This writer believes African Americans will never support Trump on a large scale. I believe Trump has a good chance of doing very well with all minorities except African Americans. My reasoning for believing this is African Americans in my view have never shed its slave dependency mentality.

Due to this dependency mentality in my view African

Insight On Trumpism And The Only Thing That Can Save USA From Total Doom

Americans see the Democratic Party as its livelihood provider instead of feeling responsible for its own survival as individuals and as a community. And that loyalty bond can't be broken its like a child's dependency on its parents for survival.

The only way this locked-in dependency can be shed or overcome is for African Americans to be forced to stand on there own two feet. But, our destructive liberal created welfare state will never force anyone to be truly responsible and accountable let alone be forced to stand on there own two feet.
SIRMANS LOG: 29 AUGUST 2015, 2306 HOURS.

THERE IS AN OLD SAYING:
"No guts. No glory". This writer for one is so glad to see someone come along that in a positive manner takes this saying to heart, because that is what it is going to take to defeat liberalism, which has all but totally destroyed this great nation.

In free societies only a true free market place economy can keep liberalism at bay and under control, unlike in an authoritarian society that uses the iron fist to control liberalism. Almost every crime or vice imaginable in the USA is running rampant and the law can't even keep drugs out of the prisons let alone stop hardly anything else.

The most powerful thing in a free society is not the law but a true free market place economy. The USA economy today is not real or true but a phony weak P.... A true free market place economy can't exist with any kind of forced government wage or price control in effect; anything else is phony and unreal, period. Before you can get control over culture rot,

Insight On Trumpism And The Only Thing That Can Save USA From Total Doom

moral decay, crime, vice, and the like's first liberalism must be faced down and subdued.

Right now in the USA liberalism is out of control. And the only way to save the great USA is to get liberalism back under control by repealing the 1938 minimum wage law. Fiddling with the tax system or anything else is an exercise in futility; liberalism will see this great country in hell first before it will slacken its death grip on this great nation.

SIRMANS LOG: 21 AUGUST 2015, 1555 HOURS.

The pundits and talking heads are all over the map on why the Trump Express seems to be at cruising speed and even extending its lead. The lead reason they are saying is the public wants non-politicians and new comers. And to some degree I think there may be some truth there.

However, I think it is something much more basic that Trump is exercising here. I think Trump is only displaying good character and being man enough to stand up for his true beliefs. In my view it is just that simple which earns genuine trust and respect from the people even if they disagree with his tactics.

In this day of scientific polling almost every politician is pandering to the people and they know it. So when a man comes along with the issues and the moral high ground at his back that strong character shows through and people trust and respect that.

The people knows Trump is not pandering, he is teaching and educating which makes a world of difference to the people on an emotional level. I'm not going to get all long winded on this matter. I think this

Insight On Trumpism And The Only Thing That Can Save USA From Total Doom

whole Trump phenomenal boils down to just strong character, which too few seem to recognize today.

Before the arch-evil 1938 socialist minimum wage law destroyed the USA true free market place economy our economy would kick ass and that kept liberalism at bay and under control. That is because any wage or price control handicaps a free market place economy where it no longer has the purging power to discipline itself or the people.

Now liberalism is out of control and almost no survival tools are left to save this great country. The road to hell is paved with good intentions, but human beings are not motivated by good handout liberal intentions they are motivated by a response to reward or punishment.

You help someone help themselves otherwise you create a dependent and mentally destroy a good human being sometimes for life. Liberalism and our welfare state have all but totally destroyed this great predominant Christian nation.

It is impossible for the USA to survive very much longer unless this 1938 minimum wage law is repealed. With my almost super natural wisdom I can be wrong on a lot of things but without a doubt the must to get rid of the evil 1938 socialist minimum wage law is not one of them.

No country can survive very long with government providing for more than the military and a very few other essential services only, it is just impossible. The evil minimum wage law allows for government to

inflate the currency and provide for its own
destruction.

This evil 1938 socialist minimum wage law must be
repealed for the USA to survive, otherwise the USA
collapses back to the stone age, period.
SIRMANS LOG: 14 AUGUST 2015, 2317 HOURS.

ADD ON #1
I understand it but 98 percent of the American
population doesn't that it is impossible for the USA to
survive much longer with government as a super
provider welfare state. So, the key is a way must be
found to get the American people back to being
providers for themselves.

Repealing the evil 1938 socialist minimum wage law
will in a controlled manner start that process of
empowering the people back in charge of their own
survival. And I have the God given wisdom to know
until this wolf in sheep clothing free market place wage
control killer is repealed nothing can save the USA no
matter what anyone says or does.

You can take what I say with a grain of salt or you can
take it to the bank, but I guarantee you history will
prove me right on this. Sure, much of what I write is to
the extreme and tough love, but I am all about
survival baby, not just feel good policy and going the
way of the Great Auk.
SIRMANS LOG: 14 AUGUST 2015, 1154 HOURS.

ADD ON #2
I, great writer Freddie L Sirmans Sr. see Trump as a
great trailblazer. Reminds me of "Give-em hell," Harry!
A supporter yelled "Give-em hell," Harry! Truman

Insight On Trumpism And The Only Thing That Can Save USA From Total Doom

replied, "I don't give them hell. I just tell the truth about them and they think its hell". That is what Trump is doing just being unafraid to tell the truth. I say give-um hell, Trump!

Sure, Trump is blazing a huge trail and USA politics will not return to just the same old business as usual in my view. However, as a writer of almost super natural wisdom I repeat, the cold reality is the USA is far past the point of no return morally, culturally, and financially to be saved unless a miracle occurs.

When a house foundation is decayed and rotten to the core that house can't be saved unless it's foundation is rebuilt from scratch. The USA house foundation nuclear and extended family system is in almost total ruins and there has never been a society that survived with that being the case.

We have same sex marriages and mass killing of future unborn babies in the womb as the norm. We have over 95 percent of the USA general population looking to government as their savior when it doesn't produce one red cent. The financing of everything the government has or gets was seized from the private sector.

The only guaranteed thing that can possibly save the USA at this late stage is to repeal the arch-evil 1938 socialist minimum wage law. But, only a miracle can make that happen when 98 percent of the USA population fail to understand the 1938 minimum wage law is a wolf in sheep clothing and a free market place economy killer.

In my view ever since 1938 the USA economy has been a weak powerless P.... with no purging power to

Insight On Trumpism And The Only Thing That Can Save USA From Total Doom

discipline itself or the nation all due to the evil 1938 minimum wage law. God save the great USA.
SIRMANS LOG: 15 AUGUST 2015, 1131 HOURS.

ADD ON #3
Here is another thing, Trump is perceived as bigger than life. Look at how people worship Hollywood and the Stars. There is just something in our human makeup that causes most of us to be impressed with power and individuals that seems bigger than life.

It reminds me of what some of the early American evangelist's discovered and said: Those like Father Divine and others discovered that as a rule being just plain and ordinary no matter how good your message was it would not get you a great following.

But, on the other hand as a rule when one projected an image of expensiveness, a lot pomp and extravaganza with flashy dressing and cars it tended to result in a much bigger following. There seems to be something in the human spirit that attracts them to things bigger than life.

Just Look at the Brits, No one beats the British in ceremony, pomp, extravaganza, and that sort of thing. And this little island nation single-handed ruled almost the entire world for many years. So, I'm telling you human being loves this bigger than life stuff. People and nations that are good at this sort of thing pack an awesome wallop.

In my view never count someone like Trump out. Plus, the secret and power behind all of this is: There is no better way of teaching and learning than through ceremonies and rituals, especially for the young, they just eats it up and soaks it all in. Look at the effect rap

Insight On Trumpism And The Only Thing That Can Save USA From Total Doom

has on the young, they see the star's as bigger than life.

SIRMANS LOG: 16 AUGUST 2015, 1730 HOURS.

IS ARMAGEDDON NEAR???
CAN A MIRACLE SAVE THE USA FROM TOTAL DOOM? INTELLIGENCE VERSUS RAW WISDOM

I don't know why I had the urge to write this article. Maybe it is out of frustration more than anything else. Even though I know I am right, still sometimes I wonder and have doubts about my God given wisdom and sanity in terms of what I write and believe.

This thing they call judgment thinking has somewhat haunted me ever since childhood. The ability to separate self and emotions from a problem and bore through fog and side issues right to the core has been with me ever since I was a young child.

Even when I hoed vegetable rows on our farm as a ten or eleven year old my dad and older sister Betty would criticize the way I did my rows. They would say why couldn't you hoe your rows like ours. Even then I did things in an organized and systematic way and to me my rows looked and seemed to be better but they disagreed.

Even today with the books I write I know ninety five percent of the USA population will never believe or understand what the hell I'm writing. It is not because my writing is complicated it is just the opposite, many people see most of my writing as simple nonsense babble and even stupidity.

Many years ago I read a book and can't even remember the title or who the author was but I do

Insight On Trumpism And The Only Thing That Can Save USA From Total Doom

remember the author talking about meaning. He went on to say just a dot on a piece of paper may not mean anything to others looking at it, but the meaning and wisdom behind who put it there may have took a life time (paraphrased).

As to my self, I'm not educated, brilliant, or highly intelligent, in fact I'm the slow plodder type, but once I understand the basics my slow climb takes me high up on the mountain top. And I definitely understand's the basics of an economy, which the USA general population does not.

I think anyone with any depth and even a weak survival instinct knows that our great USA is in serious survival trouble with eighteen trillion in debt.

The problem is can the USA be saved with our individual freedom still intact. However, not everyone thinks the country needs saving, especially liberals. I'm one that can't figure out if liberals are shallow because they are liberal or liberal because they are shallow.

Anyway, many a liberals have become conservative over night when a mugger slammed one up side the head or some other dreadful thing happened to one personally. Otherwise, what's happening to someone else can't seem to get through to his or her shallow brains.

Now, back to simple things that sometimes have a deep meaning like the dot I previously mention. Here is a short sentence that I have dwelled on for the last two years or so and what several of my latest books are about.

The sentence I'm talking about is: The arch-evil 1938

Insight On Trumpism And The Only Thing That Can Save USA From Total Doom

socialist minimum wage law must be repealed. Maybe I'm a fool, dummy, idiot, or just plain stupid, but I for real believe the 1938 minimum wage law paved the way for the doomsday welfare state the USA have today. The come about of the 1938 minimum wage law is what has caused the destruction of the nations moral, spiritual, and family values.

Here is the reasons behind my beliefs on this minimum wage law: From a pure economic understanding point of view there is no way a true free market place will allow inflation or a welfare state to get off the ground. A true free market economy has the ability to reset back to zero wages and prices and purge out inflation and without inflation a welfare state can't get off the ground.

You see, a true free market place economy is 100 percent totally controlled by the private sector, period. Bartering and trade is the foundation of every private sector economy and adding a currency takes it from there.

In hard and troubling times, especially during the great depression there was a mixture of bartering and currency use, many doctors were paid with farm products. But, in my view the main advantage of a free market place free of government control is the economy has discipline power through purging to reset back to zero if necessary.

A merchant couldn't charge more than the consumers had the ability to pay and stay in business. Sure, before the minimum wage law came along the system had many problems. You had the boom and bust cycle coming along every seven years or so, but what those that lack wisdom failed to realize is nature must have a

Insight On Trumpism And The Only Thing That Can Save USA From Total Doom

way to purge out and get rid of moral decay and culture rot.

Now, after nearly eighty years moral decay and culture rot is so powerful that without a miracle it may take going back to the Stone Age to get rid of the waste and rot. Before the 1938 minimum wage law not only did the USA economy purge out financial waste and rot it protected our moral, spiritual, and family values, too.

In 1938 the last of the "New deal" programs was enacted, the Fair Labor Standard of 1938 (FLSA). Wham! In one stroke for the first time in the USA existence an economy that had always been 100 percent able to operate under private control, now all private property rights, business production, and business distribution has flipped to 100 percent under government control.

There-after all wages and prices paid would be what the government said they would be. The minimum wage act took away the USA economy ability to reset back to zero thereby eliminating its purging power to discipline itself or the nation. Ever since that day the USA economy has been too weak to safeguard the nations culture, morals, and spiritual values.

By destroying the USA economy's ability to reset back to zero and purge out inflation the shallow minded liberals was free to tax and spend to kingdom come. Now the liberals with very little resistance has by taxing and spending made so many government dependents and left the nation 18 trillion in debt only a miracle can save the nation from total doom.

Insight On Trumpism And The Only Thing That Can Save USA From Total Doom

Still, I love-um all they are good Americans its just that they shouldn't be in charge and running things, period. However, even with a miracle the only way the USA can possible be saved is to first repeal the arch-evil 1938 socialist minimum wage law, period.

I don't believe nothing else no matter what it is can save the great USA until first this arch-evil minimum wage law is gotten rid of once and for all. That is just the way it is, sorry, I call it as I see it.

There is no long time survival for any nation with same sex marriages, mass killing of future unborn babies in the womb, and endless means of birth control galore. Don't shoot me the messenger, I don't make any rules, Mother Nature does.

Order, order, order, we have just about lost our great USA when far too many people today justify physical resisting law enforcement. Sure, there are some abuse and always has been, but never forget civilization cannot exist without law and order first and on the spot. Take up your grievances later.

Our doomsday welfare state has made far too many people feel like kings unto themselves with special entitlements and pampered treatment. Armageddon must be near.
SIRMANS LOG: 28 JULY 2015, 2305 HOURS.

HAVE RINO'S SECRETLY TAKEN OVER THE REPUBLICAN PARTY???

Insight On Trumpism And The Only Thing That Can Save USA From Total Doom

I BELIEVE THE RINO'S IN HIGH PLACES AND GLEEFUL LIBERAL MEDIA IS JUST ABOUT FED UP WITH "THE DONALD." AND WILL TRY TO TAKE HIM DOWN AT ALL COST.

GOP INFESTED WITH RINO's:ANOTHER PREDICTION BY THIS GREAT WRITER MAY COME TRUE.

FIRST SOME WORDS OF WISDOM FROM THE GREAT WRITER AND THINKER.

Tax, tax, tax, naive, naive, naive, is I the only one left with any real wisdom, here. Flat tax, value added tax, sales tax, and on and on, but the fact is it really doesn't matter which tax system is better or worse. No tax system can support a welfare state or any government in the role of social and family provider very long.

Government survives on profit by taking it from the private sector. It takes profit from the private sector in the form of taxes or seizes property and auctions it off for the profit. Government has the power and once government becomes a social and family provider its going to take what it needs as a provider no matter what form of tax collection system it uses.

The fact is government should never become a permanent social and family provider in the first place. Sure, temporary government assistant as a last resort is not a threat, but to make it permanent is a poison pill.

The founding fathers did everything possible to erect barriers to limit the size of government, but once government becomes a super provider it pays the cost

Insight On Trumpism And The Only Thing That Can Save USA From Total Doom

to be the boss. Economically speaking, boom and bust cycles are natural and comes with the territory.

That is why a strong nuclear and extended family system, good moral and spiritual values, and adequate emergency bartering capacity with many, many small farmers and home gardeners are a must.

Any nation with the above mention tools in place can withstand and ride out any bust cycle until a new boom cycle kick in. But, God help a nation without those tools when the bust cycle hit, it could mean back to the Stone Age. The boom and bust cycle is part of nature the same as the life and death cycle.

Sure, man is able to delay the cycle but nature dictate at some point the cycle must be completed, and the sad part is the longer the delay the more severe the bust cycle will be. And anyone that thinks I'm off my rocker is a fool in my view.

Even at this late stage a true genuine free market place economy can work miracles, but, a minimum wage law bounds and gags an economy and takes away it's power to discipline itself. Unless the USA repeals the evil 1938 socialist minimum wage law the USA has no chance of surviving the big bust cycle looming on the horizon.

Almost everyone thinks the law is the most powerful thing in a free nation but it is not, the economy is the most powerful thing in a free nation. The reason we have morals, values, and the inner fabric of the nation coming apart is because the USA has had an unreal phony inflated P.... of an economy ever since the arch evil 1938 socialist minimum wage law was enacted by the liberals.

Insight On Trumpism And The Only Thing That Can Save USA From Total Doom

Without the minimum wage law a real genuine free market place economy would have through purging protected the nations proper norms and traditions. Today our norms have become extreme and perverted, ISMDH (I shake my damn head). And that leave our young, which is 100 percent of our future totally unprepared for survival.

Sure, the USA has always had severe problems throughout its existence but never was its culture and family values ripped apart until after the evil 1938 socialist minimum wage law bounded and gagged the real USA economy.
SIRMANS LOG: 01 JULY 2015, 2317 HOURS.

GAY MARRIAGE UPROAR: GREAT WRITER SPEAKS BRIEFLY ON THE MATTER
Ok, Ok, I see and hear all of the uproar about gay marriage, but the fact is it matters very little either way because the USA and western civilization is doomed anyway unless a miracle takes place. What most people don't realize is there is a proven reason for all norms and traditions.

There is a reason why every society known to man has rituals and ceremonies. Until our welfare state came along in the USA our norms and traditions were well maintained and protected. Anyone like me with a strong survival instinct knows without being told that survival of the species is totally 100 percent dependent on the young and unborn.

Insight On Trumpism And The Only Thing That Can Save USA From Total Doom

Therefore rituals, ceremonies, marriages, norms, and traditions all are for the raising and teaching of the young. And there has never been and never will be an institution more suitable for the raising and teaching of the young than marriage under the umbrella of a nuclear and extended family system.

Anything no matter what it is that threatens this evolutionary process is a threat to human survival. And if man fails to protect this evolutionary process, Mother Nature will definite step in soon. And mother nature's way of dealing with the situation is resetting modern civilization back to the Stone Age, we'll find out soon. The USA is living on borrowed time, economically-wise, morally-wise, and spiritually-wise.

In the USA mostly liberal hogwash is the norms being instilled in our young today, which makes it impossible for this great nation to survive very much longer, period.

Once our welfare state became a super social and family provider it never gave a damn about maintaining and protecting proper norms and traditions. And now here we are today in the great USA with a generation of citizens that don't know their ass from a hole in the ground in terms of raw bare bone survival.

The only thing that can save the USA is to repeal the Arch evil 1938 socialist minimum wage law. That in itself won't directly save the USA, but it will start a process of getting rid of our inflated phony economy so

Insight On Trumpism And The Only Thing That Can Save USA From Total Doom

a true free market place economy can kick in and allow the people to take back control of their lives.

I could analyze much, much more but enough said, I think you get the point.

SIRMANS LOG: 27 JUNE 2015, 2220 HOURS.

SUPREME COURT RULING ON SUBSIDIES WAS ACTUALLY A GOD SEND TO THE REPUBLICAN PARTY EVEN IF THEY WON'T ADMIT IT

I will make this very brief, there has never been a society headed toward total financial collapse that has ever changed course, power concedes nothing and always goes down with the ship.

Recognized or not, it is a fact that it is impossible for the nation to afford Obamacare, yet we proceed on. You can't get blood out of a turnip, and you can't have health care for long when very, very few can afford it.

In the grand theme of things this latest Supreme Court decision really doesn't matter because the USA is far too far down the socialist road to be saved without a miracle anyway.

In life there is really no such thing as free, one way or another everything has a price even every decision we make.

This recent Supreme Court decision about subsidies was actually a blessing in disguise to the Republican Party, because this insane Obamacare debacle is very soon going to start dishing out a lot of dreadful financial pain, but the scheming irresponsible liberals won't have the Republican Party to blame and kick

Insight On Trumpism And The Only Thing That Can Save USA From Total Doom

around on this due to the supreme's ruling.

The USA economy is already on the brink of a total collapse with 18 trillion in debt and there is no possible way our economy can survive Obamacare in my view. The USA is doomed as a free nation unless our arch evil 1938 socialist minimum wage law is repealed. But, we have 98 percent of the nation thinking the minimum wage is not only a good thing but the only thing that matters and ought to be raised.

The only solution to save the USA at this late moral decay and culture rot stage is to get rid of the minimum wage law entirely and to have no wage or price controls what so ever, then the free market place will be free to set it's own wages and prices without the heavy hand of the government thumb on the scale.

Otherwise, this whole USA and world economy is going to soon collapse and take us all back to the Stone Age. All of that being said, as for the USA, only a divine act of God can bring about a repeal of this arch evil 1938 socialist minimum wage law. Glory be to God. Long live a free America. Hallelujah.

Political I am an independent, but I see the Republican Party as the only hope of saving the USA from total doom. After the Supreme's recent ruling on subsides to me it looks like the stars, the Gods, and destiny itself are all pointing to a republican Trifecta win in November 2016.

And if that does happen the republicans will have the power to once and for all repeal and put a dagger through the heart of this arch evil 1938 socialist minimum wage law. I believe that is the only thing

Insight On Trumpism And The Only Thing That Can Save USA From Total Doom

that can save the USA and western civilization from total doom.

However, they think I am a total nut case, and right now the odds are 100 percent they will never do something like that. Never the less if they do win a Trifecta in November 2016 no one can ever say the republicans never had a chance to save the USA and western civilization from total doom.
SIRMANS LOG: 25 JUNE 2015, 1154 HOURS.

IS THIS WRITER A BLOOMING IDIOT OR A MAN OF GREAT WISDOM? TRUE OR FALSE, MAKE YOUR COMMENT AT THE BOTTOM.
As a great writer, deep thinker, and unsung super achiever I feel more and more of my predictions are beginning to come to past.

Especially my constant drum beating to no end that any minimum wage law is evil and means death to a true genuine free market place economy. But, it is like a lone voice hollering in the wilderness, everything falls on deaf ears, no one is interesting in taking my bitter medicine.

The USA, Greece, Western Europe, and much more of the world uses the minimum wage to inflate currencies and prop up phony economies. A phony economy is the only way a welfare state can survive because without a minimum wage law a true free market place economy will purge out inflation and keep it out.

Insight On Trumpism And The Only Thing That Can Save USA From Total Doom

I'm not going to go into details on the damage the minimum wage law does to a free market place economy in this article, that can be found in the many, many books I have written. No one asks me and no one is going to take my advice anyway. However, my advice to all welfare states is get rid of any minimum wage law now before it is too late.

When everything collapses it will be too late then except back to the Stone Age. With no minimum wage law in place the people are free to open millions of small businesses, hire each other, trade and barter with each other, and in effect save themselves and the nation, too. Right now in the USA and other welfare states that is impossible, too much red tape.

The minimum wage law is only the first of thousands of laws, licenses, permits and other road blocks unimaginable. Today in the USA almost everyone is depending on the government or someone other than self for his or her survival. And the people are going to be lost when big government, big business, and this colossal welfare state soon collapses.

The first problem is 95 percent of the USA population doesn't believe that something so unimaginable can happen. It is not only going to happen, but I'm here to tell you it is not as far away as we think. No one knows the day or hour when the collapse is going to occur but to the wise all of the signs are present now.

Greece is only the tip of the spear in my view.
SIRMANS LOG: 23 JUNE 2015, 2213 HOURS.

Insight On Trumpism And The Only Thing That Can Save USA From Total Doom

SPARE THE ROD YOU SPOIL THE CHILD!

I, Freddie L Sirmans Sr. as a writer of almost supernatural wisdom believe that is just as true today as it was 2000 years ago. On this article I'm writing I haven't done any research and don't feel a need to on the things I am about to say. I already know there is an exception to everything in life no matter what it is.

In general as a rule my statements will hold true enough, and that is good enough for me. "You raise up a child the way he/she should be and when he gets older he will not depart, and if he should stray most likely at some point he will return to his raising."

Why should anyone expect a child to be responsible and accountable when he/she has never been conditioned to be responsible and accountable? There is nothing that will instill a stronger conscience in a child than carpal punishment, but it should only be used fairly and as a last resort.

Today we have people committing suicide in some cases almost at epidemic levels. Today we have far more people committing horrendous crimes and murder. Today we have far too many people growing up on all kinds of mind-altering drugs, both legal and illegal. And I could go on and on.

However, I see one common thread going throughout all of these sad situations. That common thread I'm speaking of is very few if any of these people growing up ever felt the sting of hard lick on their ass for improper behavior.

Disagree if you may, but the fact remains, human beings respond and is motivated by reward or

Insight On Trumpism And The Only Thing That Can Save USA From Total Doom

punishment and talk is only rhetoric. Plus, good and evil is just two sides of the same coin. I rest my case. **SIRMANS LOG: 22 JUNE 2015, 0143 HOURS.**

WRITER BELIEVES WITHIN THE NEXT 17 MONTHS THERE WILL BE AN ALL OUT LIBERALS ASSULT ON THE 2ND AMMENDMENT.
Don't be a fool, don't be a fool, and don't be a fool! The liberals are on the brink of totally destroying the greatest, richest, freest, and most prosperous nation to ever exist.

In my view they have just about destroyed the USA by creating our welfare state. But, a welfare state could never have survived this long without first depending on a phony inflated currency.

When the liberals enacted the arch evil 1938 socialist minimum wage law that blocked the economy's ability to discipline itself by being able to freely purge and reset wages and prices back to zero. Of course no one is going to work for zero that would be slavery, but the seller and buyer should set wages and prices never the government.

Thereby without the economy's ability to purge inflation and reset prices and wages back to zero the liberals have been able to tax and spend and inflate our currency to no end. This 1938 evil law in one sweep for the first time gave the federal government absolute power over all United States private property rights and private business production and distribution.

Thereafter, the government would have the final say on all price and wage transactions in the nation, private or otherwise. The real miracle working power in

31

Insight On Trumpism And The Only Thing That Can Save USA From Total Doom

a free market place economy is its purging ability to get rid of waste and inefficiency regardless of who you know or b... The minimum wage law acts as a purge inhibitor and leaves a free market place economy with no way to protect itself or the nations culture and morals values.

Beginning with the enacting of the 1938 minimum wage law the USA economy could no longer purge out inflation. That is why ever since the 1938 minimum wage law the USA has slowly been going to hell in a hand basket. Now, every kinky and negative anti-survival special interest group imaginable is out of control and running wild.

They now have the coalition power to bring this great nation to its knees. Almost eighty years after the enacting of the 1938 minimum wage law only one tiny thread is preventing the liberals from administrating the final coup de grace. Except for this last tiny thread the liberals today would destroy the last bastion of true individual freedom left in world today.

That tiny little thread I'm talking about is the 2nd amendment. And I believe within the next seventeen months the liberals once and for all are going to pounce for a kill to try to take away our guns. Will the Gods allow it to happen, we'll see.

I will sum up by saying this: If I had to pick just one thing as the cause of the USA coming destruction, It would be the enactment of this arch evil 1938 socialist minimum wage law. And I don't believe anything can save the USA until this law is repealed, even if no one else believes that except me.

Nothing on earth has the power to produce jobs,

Insight On Trumpism And The Only Thing That Can Save USA From Total Doom

wealth, and abundance like a true kick ass free market place economy. Repeal this evil 1938 socialist minimum wage law to set our economy free again to set its own wages and prices not the government. Repeal this evil law and save this great USA nation, for Christ sake, people. Hallelujah!!!

SIRMANS LOG: 19 JUNE 2015, 1430 HOURS.

WHAT WAS THE FIRST THING GEORGE WASHINGTON SAID WHEN HE RODE UP TO THE WHITE HOUSE: WHOA! WHAT WILL BE THE FIRST THING THE ESTABLISHMENT WILL SAY WHEN THE TRUMP EXPRESS ENDS UP AT THE WHITE HOUSE: HOLY COW, UNBELIEVABLE! SIRMANS LOG: 12 AUGUST 2015, 2044 HOURS.

HAVE RINO'S SECRETLY TAKEN OVER THE REPUBLICAN PARTY???

CAN THE REPUBLICAN RINO'S AND GLEEFUL SOCIALIST LIBERAL MEDIA STOP THE TRUMP EXPRESS???

WHAT DO YOU THINK OF THIS WRITER'S ANALYSIS???

THE TRUMP PHENOMENAL:
I, Freddie L Sirmans Sr. man of great almost supernatural wisdom and deep deep creative thinking has decided to weigh in on the Trump presidential candidacy. As a self-made writer I very seldom comment on individuals.

However, I think Trump entering the 2016 presidential race is so profound that it has the potential to shake up politics in this nation more than anything in the last

Insight On Trumpism And The Only Thing That Can Save USA From Total Doom

century. And a word to the wise, not taking this man serious may be the biggest mistake anyone can make.

I believe his candidacy is going to effect the liberals and democrats even more so than the republicans, simply because he has the issues, moral high ground, and headwinds all at his back. Which means the more the predominant liberal news media attacks him the bigger and more popular he will become.

But, my guess is the liberal news media will avoid attacking him head-on issue-wise and instead pound away on pretending he is not a serious candidate and whatever he says is not to be taken seriously.

In my view the liberal news media just steam rolled over the last three republican presidential candidate losers, but now they have finally in their eyes met a foe that will stand toe to toe and refuse to back down, high drama pending.

No pun intended, I think Trump is not a man to "Beat around the bushes. I think Trump is not afraid and is going to constantly, no pun intended, beat the bushes. And if nothing more beating the bushes" long enough will eventually drive the political snakes from both political parties out into the open.

Also, I believe its going to make it a lot harder for the RINO's to hide their true colors. I see some republicans already becoming very emotional when talking about Trump. I believe if Trump doesn't cave like the last three republican presidential candidate losers he is going to make believers out of a lot of people including me. I never though he would ever run in the first place.

And another thing, they are going to hound him to no end on details, which is a trap because if he is suckered into that they got him. Everyone knows the

Insight On Trumpism And The Only Thing That Can Save USA From Total Doom

Dem's are going to promise the moon and back and tax and spend to kingdom come, but when have they ever gave details in advance?

Instead of trying to pander to the poll results republicans need to stand for what will save the country and focus on educating the public. I know without a doubt that the republican base and most of the country will never vote against someone totally committed to lower taxes, more jobs, and strong national defense, period.

Instead the republican candidates in the last three presidential elections has tried to out pander the liberals, which is scatter brained thinking in my view. Limiting and dwelling on three or less things then people get it, but chasing votes you'll never get and being all over the map means no one knows what you are selling or what you really stands for.

It is all about building and turning out your base, the Dem's know this, that is why they keep winning presidential elections.

Reality is reality and fact is fact, and the reality and fact is Trump is saying a lot of things a lot of people are agreeing with. That concludes my analysis.

I give the Dem's credit for the fact they have no shame or regret when going down holding on to what they believe in, they double down and there is never any talk of changing into something they are not concerning their base.

On the other hand, there should never be any shame or regret for the republican party going down fighting for lower taxes, more jobs, and strong national defense. Instead the Republican Party is trying to be all things to all people, which end up pleasing no one, and leaving the base with candidates they don't trust

Insight On Trumpism And The Only Thing That Can Save USA From Total Doom

except the lesser of two evils.

Now, on a personal basis, I don't want to end up begging on the streets, but I will go down holding on to what I write and believe in even if no one ever agree with me. A many of times I have felt cursed with wisdom that no one but me seems to see. And I have wondered why do I keep preaching to deaf ears.

No one seems to be interesting in my bitter medicine, yet there is a drive to fight on for my survival and that of my nation. I don't know if it is destiny, fate, or insanity, but, deep down in my soul I feel some way some how my seemingly wasted effort is not in vain **SIRMANS LOG: 17 JUNE 2015, 1531 HOURS.**

PS: I see the anticipated coming drama and excitement with Trump in the 2016 presidential race as very refreshing. However, I feel I must add my own belief as a writer of almost supernatural wisdom for the record.

Until the evil 1938 socialist minimum wage law is repealed I don't believe it is possible for the great USA to be saved, period.

PS#2: "THE DONALD RIDES AGAIN."

PS#3: One may not agree with "The Donald," but the political process in the USA may need shaking up. The USA is 18 trillion in debt and our economy could collapse at any moment. Our nuclear and extended family system is in ruins. Our good moral and spiritual values are in ruins.

We have no emergency back-up bartering capacity with small farmers and home gardeners to survive on

Insight On Trumpism And The Only Thing That Can Save USA From Total Doom

and regroup-with if the economy collapses, or any big disaster strikes. If anything big and bad happened to the USA it could be the end because we have let the welfare state destroy all of our must tools for human survival.

Who knows why something's happens. The good "Lord works in mysterious ways." Repeal the arch-evil 1938 socialist minimum wage law or the USA perishes.

I don't know and no one else knows why this "Trump" phenomenal is so powerful and dramatic, but, one thing I do know beyond a shadow of doubt is only a miracle can save the USA from total doom. Is there some kind of fate or destiny message in all of this high drama?

During the Great depression: The USA nuclear and extended family system was strong, reliable, and healthy. The USA morals and spiritual values were good, solid, and above reproach. The USA had masses of small farmers and home gardeners that provided enough emergency back-up bartering capacity to feed and save the nation.

However, this time around we are left with practical none of the above mentions must have survival tools. I believe the iron fist will be used to kill millions just to bring about order, but even that won't be enough due to no survival tools left to rebuild with. Back to the Stone Age may be the final destination.

This is all fiction and the exercise of my overly active imagination, please dismiss.
SIRMANS LOG: 19 JULY 2015, 142 HOURS.

PS#4: You know what Dick Nixon said when one of his

Insight On Trumpism And The Only Thing That Can Save USA From Total Doom

sidekicks was caught misbehaving, "sure, he is an S.O.B. but he is our S.O.B." And I doubt there will be any serious changes in the polls involving the McCain case. The whole USA political process is being shaken-up to the very core, and we'll all just have to wait and see what eventually comes out in the wash. God save the good old USA.

SIRMANS LOG: 20 JULY 2015, 2241 HOURS.

WRITER FREDDIE L SIRMANS SR. CRIES OUT IN PAIN FOR THE FUTURE OF HIS BELOVED COUNTRY THE USA.

It is so sad what the welfare state and liberal news media has done to this great nation the USA. Order, order, order, and more order, it is impossible to have an orderly and civilized society without order.

Our liberal induced welfare state has turned much of the USA into a needy greedy, self-centered, uncivilized, unforgiving, and ungrateful people in my opinion. It just confirms what most people with real wisdom already knows, if one doesn't have to struggle for it, life and everything in it becomes cheap and taken for granted.

Self-sacrificing and some time giving up a right for a wrong is becoming rare and rarer, now, it is all about me, me first, I want mine, I want it all, what kind of society has we become?

Most of the young today has never faced cold tough hard discipline that demands obedience now, no sass, and no back talk, just obey and act now. Our welfare state has allowed a false reality to come about in this great nation and now the piper must be paid, and

Insight On Trumpism And The Only Thing That Can Save USA From Total Doom

believe me we as a nation is about to pay dearly in blood, sweat, and tears. Just keep on living we'll see.

I believe the USA and western civilization itself is in the final stages of their life ending cancer-ridden welfare states. Enough said, no one want to hear my bitter medicine, I will leave you with this: In my view no form of government has ever existed that was more self-destructive than a welfare state.

Not even a pure communist or socialist state completely destroys the very foundation of human survival itself like a welfare state does, given enough time a welfare state will totally destroy the nuclear and extended family system and leave no tools in place to rebuild upon. The USA and much of western civilization is past the point of no return. God have mercy.

In the end a welfare states leaves almost nothing to rebuild upon, it leaves the nuclear and extended family system in ruins, it leaves good moral and spiritual values in ruins, and it leaves no emergency bartering capacity with small farmers and home gardeners to speak of. No tools, practical nothing is left, its literally is back to the Stone Age.
SIRMANS LOG: 15 JUNE 2015, 1356 HOURS.

PS: Anyone that thinks that our own welfare state wasn't somehow behind the recent hacking of government personnel files must believe in the tooth fairy in my view.
SIRMANS LOG: 12 JUNE 2015, 1001 HOURS.

NOTE: UNCONSTITUTIONALLY BUREAUCRATIC LAWS ARE BREEDING CONTEMPT FOR THE LAW ITSELF.

Insight On Trumpism And The Only Thing That Can Save USA From Total Doom

Respect and obeying the law is extremely important for the survival of a free nation. Yet, we have a law that punishes one for how they withdraw their own money from the bank.

I think that kind of a law breeds contempt and disrespect for the law itself, period. Sure, no law is going to please everyone, but what happen to its better to let the guilty go free than to punish one innocent individual. What has we become, has the almighty dollar took over our souls.

TOO MANY REPUBLICANS TODAY ACT MORE LIKE WANNA BE DEMOCRATS.
The attack dog liberal news media has shamed republicans off of the three things that have always won them presidential elections. The three things are lower taxes, more jobs, and strong national defense.

The founding fathers designed this great country as a republic for those seeking elective office to educate the people on what is in the best interest of the survival of the country, not to surrender to phony polls on what greedy, emotional, uninformed, and irrational voters want.

A true statesman will go down fighting for what is right for the survival of his/her country, not just to gain or keep power and let the country go to hell in a hand basket. Folks, don't hate me for what I believe. Let me explain, politically speaking I am a freethinking independent.

I didn't set out to favor any one political party my sole interest is acknowledging the best chance of the USA survival as I see it. Forgive me, but with the liberals

Insight On Trumpism And The Only Thing That Can Save USA From Total Doom

and democrats I see no chance of the USA surviving. Again, forgive me, still with the conservatives and republicans I see almost no chance of the USA surviving, but even with a flicker some hope exist.

The fore mention three things are very simple and may not seem important in today's debt ridden welfare state, but they are still republicans winners. If Dole, McCain, and Romney had locked on to them three simple things I believe they would have won.

The liberal news media can't defeat one that locks on to lower taxes, more jobs, and strong national defense. And they will never attack these three things directly, but will instead pound away for details and try to brand one as mean and uncaring, only a statesman can withstand the pressure.

Anyone advocating lower taxes, more jobs, and strong national defense should never be suckered into giving details, because everyone knows the Dem's are always going to tax and spend and when have they ever given details in advance.

One may not agree with the democrats but one thing is for sure, everyone knows what they stands for like it or not, they stands for bigger government and more social spending, and gives the middle finger to our soon to be $20,000,000,000,000 debt.

On the other hand, right now if you ask anyone what the last three losing republicans presidential candidates actually stood for, duh, no one knows. That is the problem with the Republican Party today, it lacks a core belief of trust for people to make a strong choice and fight for it.

Insight On Trumpism And The Only Thing That Can Save USA From Total Doom

Unless someone is prepared to make an iron stand on three or less things and not let the liberal news media keep them all over the map 2016 is going to be another loser repeat. It is a given the liberal news media is going to brand anyone that doesn't start promising goodies as mean and uncaring.

Who says people won't vote for you unless you answer every silly or unnecessary question the liberal news media may ask, no comment will get my vote every time. One can't be everything to everybody and expect to survive the liberal news media, because for every republican they are the real opponents.

With the persistence and determination of the liberal news media only an iron will can keep one locked on to lower taxes, more jobs, and strong national defense, which has always allowed republicans to win presidential elections.

Many years ago just like the democrats everyone knew exactly what republicans stood for, lower taxes, more jobs, and strong national defense. Now, the republicans acts more like wanna be democrats and is going to lose again in 2016 unless they return home to basics.
SIRMANS LOG: 30 MAY 2015, 1509 HOUR.

The all over the map strategy is already starting, and unless a republican limit at all cost to lower taxes, more jobs, and strong national defense 2016 will be a lost cause. Focusing on side issues like entitlement issues, voter fraud, illegal immigrate driver license, and other like stuff to the Dem's is like

Insight On Trumpism And The Only Thing That Can Save USA From Total Doom

throwing a rabbit in a brier patch.

That keeps the focus off of the dire condition of the economy, lack of jobs, insane medical cost, and sky-high daily cost of living, duh. And I wouldn't be one bit surprised if the republicans fall for it again in 2016.

I must give the liberals credit, they may be shallow but they are smart enough to know that the republicans cannot defeat them for the presidency by trying to solve the entitlement-spending dilemma. And they are right; it is a fool's game in terms of becoming president of the USA.

The liberal news media will make sure the general public is kept economically ignorant and will fight tooth and nails to keep them that way. The sad part is we are going to lose our freedom and this great nation and the republicans do have the sense to know it if something is not done.

Whereas the liberals are too shallow or selfish to realize the danger and will readily go down with the ship just to gain or keep power. Lord knows, I hope I'm wrong, but I believe the USA economy is on the brink of collapsing for real.

I believe it is a given, it is going to happen, nothing is new here, everything dies or collapses at some point, otherwise there couldn't be rebirth and growth and life couldn't exist on earth.

The wise thing for the USA to do if it wants to survive past this coming collapse is free up and untie the USA economy from the evil 1938 socialist minimum wage law, that will give us a fighting chance to survive. That is the only way the people can take back charge of their lives and with a true genuine untied free market place economy nothing is impossible, freedom and the nation will survive.

If the republicans win a trifecta in 2016 they will have the power to repeal this evil 1938 socialist minimum wage law and save the last bastion of individual freedom left in the world. Otherwise, it may be another 10,000 years before individual freedom see the light of day again.

I believe the Gods are smiling down on us for this last great hope for individual freedom, it must come to past, or else.
SIRMANS LOG: 06 JUNE 2015, 0020 HOURS.

NOTE: Who really knows, there may be a divine reason how a neurotic mentally handicapped cripple misfit almost single handed can crawl out of the wood works and seize the pulse rate of this great north America giant, then sound the distress call alarm for its survival. That is no ordinary task. Hallelujah.
SIRMANS LOG: 08 JUNE 2015, 1011 HOURS.

NOTE: IS A COLLEGE DIPLOMA A MUST TODAY?
The old folks used to always say; the biggest fool of all is an educated fool. And adding my opinion I think anyone that thinks a college diploma is a must to reach the pinnacle of success in today's world is a fool.

Sure, it is an advantage to have a college diploma, nobody can deny that. Plus, in certain medical and technical fields especially the S.T.E.M fields (science,

Insight On Trumpism And The Only Thing That Can Save USA From Total Doom

technology, engineering, and mathematics) its true a college diploma is a must. But, other than that it's not that big of a deal, and even the technical skills needed can be hired when one has the money and knows what he wants.

Two of the greatest computer pioneers to ever exist were not engineers, but they knew what they wanted and got it. Enough said.

SIRMANS LOG: 25 MAY 2015, 1513 HOURS

WESTERN THINKING VERSUS MIDDLE EAST REALITY:
OK, I'm going to make a very brief statement on what I think is military common sense. In every military war or conflict there are going to be people wanting to desert or run away. I think in every army it is a death sentence to desert during time of war.

Now, that being said, it takes cold harsh brutal discipline in many cases to make the odds of surviving better fighting the enemy than running away. Many armies have used divisions behind the line to shoot on sight anyone running back to safety.

I believe in certain parts of the world with many tribal and other factions only a strongman can do what it takes to make his army fight instead of running away. And until the west realizes this fact the whole thing is an exercise in futility in my view.

That is my one man's opinion; I said the same thing during the Iraq war and haven't seen noting since to

Insight On Trumpism And The Only Thing That Can Save USA From Total Doom

change my mind. However, crying over spilt milk concerning the Iraq war serves no useful purpose and is a sign of irresponsibility and weakness.
SIRMANS LOG: 24 MAY 2015, 1724 HOURS.

FINAL SOLUTION TO THE RACE AND ECONOMIC PROBLEM IN THE USA AS SEEN BY GREAT WRITER FREDDIE L SIRMANS SR., A MUST READ.

UPDATED VERSION: AFRICAN AMERICAN EXCUSES, EXCUSES, EXCUSES, AND I'M SICK AND TIRED OF IT. WRITER ATTACKS BLACK LEADERSHIP.

Halt, stop, or brace yourself, because this great writer is fixing to let her rip, go on a tirade, rant, or what ever you may call it. OK, lets just dispense with any bull s... and just talk plain turkey. Sure, there is a lot of racism in America, always has been and always will be. Hell, I may be called a racist, but I think not.

Life is not perfect and this nation is not perfect, but it is the greatest country to ever exist in my view. I love this great country and it is the only home that I have ever known. This great country offers the most individual freedom and opportunity to ever exist on earth, and it still does in spite of our beloved tax and spends liberals, but still I love-um like a brother.

Now, as to my beloved African American race, the problem with us is too much pampering, period. Hell, I'm a neurotic mentally handicapped cripple from my childhood bed wetting days, yet I will never stoop to being just a plain excuse maker. If one accepts excuses for failure an excuse can always be found.

Sure, there may be be a good reason for an excuse, but as for my self I don't want to hear it, I only accept

46

Insight On Trumpism And The Only Thing That Can Save USA From Total Doom

results. Like a coach once said: "you show me a good loser, and I'll show you a loser." I have been counted out all of my life. For me, I have always taken responsibility for my own survival and I know beyond a shadow of doubt that otherwise I wouldn't be standing today.

Today all I hear from African American leadership is what we lack, what we don't have, we don't have jobs, and on and on. However, the question that needs to be asked is: What do we need to do for our community our selves? Duh! And they will all look at each other like helpless sheep. Number one should be how could we provide more of our own jobs in our communities.

We African Americans have our racial priorities mixed up or maybe even misplaced in my view. Everyone's priority should be immediately family first, then community, city, state, country, but ones race can never be totally ignored to fit somewhere in that order.

One must have a mental identity to know who he/she really is as a person; otherwise one could end up with no true racial identity. Something of the sort has happened to the African American race on a mass scale.

We African Americans as a race mentally see ourselves as dependent like siblings that can't do for ourselves and must be taken care of by the master. And like most siblings we are jealous and compete against each other for the master's favors. That is why you see the herd mentality and we always vote anywhere from 90 percent to 99 percent for one party in almost every election.

Insight On Trumpism And The Only Thing That Can Save USA From Total Doom

We as a race are locked into this dependent sibling psyche. It is not a bad thing, it kept the African American race alive in an almost totally hostile environment right out of slavery. However, circumstance and the nation has evolved and that type of psyche is no longer needed The only thing that can break this dependency chain is for African Americans to be forced to stand on its own two feet. Folks, I don't have anything to do with reality, I am only telling things as I see them, you have the freedom to totally disagree with anything I write and brand me a fool and idiot, so be it.

The African American race in America is awesome; we hold many of the most powerful elected offices in this great nation, from the office of president on down. There is no logical reason why African Americans can't employ at least a quarter of the jobs in its own communities, yet I doubt its over 3 percent.

For God sake, grow up African Americans, grab the bull by the horns, and learn to love all people and especially those that look like you. Now, don't you go telling me you don't have hate and contempt for those that look like you? Otherwise, why else would there be all of this mass killings in black communities?

Plus, where you spend your money proves where your first loyalty priority lies and it's certainly not with the man in the mirror. No one is expected to support a dirty greasy spoon eatery, but remember Auburn Avenue and the likes in other cities could equal the best before the welfare state came about. Now, our elites run as far as affordable away from an all black neighborhood and it is all because of our welfare state.

Insight On Trumpism And The Only Thing That Can Save USA From Total Doom

The welfare state has reduced the once proud Negro race to a bunch of government dependent siblings that are constantly at each others throat. We don't trust each other or truly respect each other and is ashamed of an all black neighborhood. And don't give me this bull excuse about high crime, the movie "Raising in the sun" proves blacks couldn't wait to get out long before crime was a problem.

If you don't love who you really are how can you expect other races to respect you. Liberalism is responsible for this sad condition and to this day still patronizes African Americans and hates nothing more than a black that's wants to be self sufficient and independent. A black conservative threatens liberals ability to keep African Americans dependent minded and self-rejecting more than anything else.

You black man, you don't truly love your own people, you mentally see yourself like your master and better than that sassy nigger that is undeserving of respect. Besides, you see that sassy nigger as a competitor against you, why should you kiss his ass and help him to get ahead, f... him, I'll spend my money where I want too, and anyone that's got a problem with that can kiss my black ass. This is the type of thinking that goes on in the minds of so many in the African American community.

The only thing that can break this locked-in African American dependency mentality is to kick the young eagle out of the welfare state nest, then it will be forced to fly on its own, that is what the mother eagle does. What I just said is not cold and uncaring, that is being prepared to survive on ones own, and not disappear off this earth when this welfare state soon

Insight On Trumpism And The Only Thing That Can Save USA From Total Doom

crashes.

The African American sad condition is the tip of the USA survival spear, or the canary in our culture mine. God save my beloved homeland. Hallelujah.

OK, OK, having aired it out and said my peace, what is the real solution to the African American problem? Anyone familiar with my work should know my constant drum beat for the only thing that can save all of America and even western civilization.

It is the economy, fool! Nothing on earth is more powerful than a genuine true free market place economy; it trumps the law and everything in terms of having and maintaining an orderly society.

However, the USA liberal socialist destroyed our true free market place economy almost eighty years ago by enacting the evil 1938 socialist minimum wage law. And the inner fabric of moral decay and culture rot along with a lack of any emergency bartering capacity has grown unabated ever since.

A true free market place economy must be absolutely free to have the power to discipline itself and the nation, the same as Mother Nature, with its supreme law of natural selection. There must be a survival need for anything in nature to exist, otherwise it starts ceasing to exist based on nature's supreme law of "Natural selection."

The enacting of the 1938 minimum wage law gave the USA government for the first time absolute power over private property rights and business production and distribution. That act for the first time allowed liberals to seize almost absolute power by operating a candy

Insight On Trumpism And The Only Thing That Can Save USA From Total Doom

store and promising the moon and back.

Before the 1938 minimum wage law it was almost impossible to inflate the USA currency because the economy had the discipline power to purge out inflation, waste, inefficiency and the likes. Now, the minimum wage law acts as a purge inhibitor and every imaginable negative anti-survival special interest group in America have grown like wild flowers unabated ever since. Mass killing's in the womb and same sex marriages are just new additions to the anti-survival paths the USA is going down.

Negative anti-survival special interest is now a swamp with the coalition power to take down this great nation. Creating our minimum wage law purge inhibitor is like trying to stop nature's life and death cycle, insane. The evil 1938 socialist minimum wage law have an almost over-powering appeal to the economically ignorant, and has all but destroyed our culture, good morals, and any capacity to barter.

A nation can't have emergency bartering capacity without enough small farmers and home gardeners, which is what got the USA through the great depression. I could go on and on with the destruction this evil 1938 socialist minimum wage law has done to this great nation.

But, I will wrap it up by saying this: Everybody and his brother has an opinion, but it is my God given destiny to let you know until the 1938 minimum wage law is repealed it is impossible for the USA to be saved. The "Final solution" is to repeal this evil law, or we perish, period.

I believe all to no avail the federal reserve and

Insight On Trumpism And The Only Thing That Can Save USA From Total Doom

politicians trying to save this welfare state beast will eventually sell the nations sovereignty, land, wealth, and mineral rights off like a hooker on the block. Plus, there is no telling what has already been sold off being $18,000,000,000,000 in debt already.

Only a handful of people know, but I seriously doubt there is any gold left at Fort Knox anymore. I can't make anybody believe me; still I believe I understand the workings of an economy as well as anyone. And I promise you this weak phony P.... of an economy the USA have today is almost as useless as tits on a boar hog in terms of saving itself or this great nation.

Repeal the 1938 minimum wage law and give the USA economy back its original power, please Sir/Madam. It is not about how much increase in wages that really count, it is about having a job to buy enough food and necessities to survive at all. What good is a higher wage if you can't afford hardy anything, duh? It won't happen overnight, but repealing the minimum wage law will wean inflation out of our currency so $1.00 will buy what $20.00 will today.

Folks, I don't have to be right on my assessment, and I even hope I'm proven wrong. Why oh Lord, why have I been blessed with so much raw wisdom, it is like a curse, I see things so clearly, why me o-lord. Writer answers that himself: Why not you. Amen.
SIRMANS LOG: 07 MAY 2015, 1328 HOURS.

LIBERAL SUICIDE SPENDING
This is a subject I decided to revisit. There is a conservative faction that wants to bring about a states

Insight On Trumpism And The Only Thing That Can Save USA From Total Doom

convention to demand the government balance it's annul budget.

On the surface having a convention to do that sounds reasonable and maybe ought to take place. Twenty years ago I probably would have jumped on the bandwagon. However, I have evolved and now realize liberalism has no boundaries or limits to what it will go to keep over spending.

Today I think any convention of the sort would more than likely cause a total disaster. The first reason is it wouldn't solve the problem. Our welfare state beast is ignoring the constitution and the law now and just adding new laws are not going to make this beast change its ways. The next reason involves human nature.

Liberals tends to be far more intelligent and smarter than conservatives but as a rule are shallow surface dwelling thinkers. The conservative's advantage has always been their focused staying power and deep sound judgment. However, there is a world of difference between today's conservatives and those in the founding fathers days.

Ever since the "New deal" and the come about of our welfare state conservatives has become almost as moral corrupted and shallow minded as liberals. It is a waste of time to pass more laws trying to force liberals to control spending.

Insight On Trumpism And The Only Thing That Can Save USA From Total Doom

They have weak survival instincts and respects no threats in spending from here to kingdom come. But, never forget liberals are not dumb or stupid, when giving up any of their own money they are the stingiest of any group. What it actually boils down to is they struggle with not being selfish to a fault, and that includes spending other people money.

Most conservatives are self-bound by morals and emotional boundaries such as guilt, shame, etc. Where as liberals tends to be far less restricted when going after something they truly want. Nothing that is within the law is going deter a liberal lion/lionness from grabbing power and keeping it.

Power is what this liberal suicide spending is all about. Social spending keeps liberals in power and no amount of morals; love of the country, or anything legal is going to stand in their way of holding on to power. Many liberals tend to be aimless but you give a liberal a cause or a goal and you got an almost unstoppable force on your hand.

If the great USA is to ever get control over suicide over spending from the liberals it can only be done with a physical barrier. So, here we go again, that means repealing the 1938 minimum wage law. Enacting that law is what took away a government-spending barrier in the first place.

That law gave liberals absolute power over private enterprise and private property rights and enable them

Insight On Trumpism And The Only Thing That Can Save USA From Total Doom

to tax spend inflate, tax spend inflate, tax spend inflate in a never-ending upward spiral. In fact I don't believe its possible for any free nation to remain free very long with liberalism and liberals at the helm.

Freedom and democracy demands a responsible and self-controlled populace to last over a hundred years in my view. The liberals seized complete control over USA private business enterprise and private property rights with the enacting of the 1938 minimum wage law.

Unless that law is repealed this nation will never remain free to 2038 let alone more than a hundred years since the law was enacted.
SIRMANS LOG: 04 MAY 2015, 2107 HOURS.

BALTIMORE SUPER MOM: I HAVE A DIFFERENT VIEWPOINT ON THAT MATTER. WHAT DO YOU THINK?

In fact this writer is out of phase with almost everything that goes on now a days. I take no joy in raining on anyone's parade or stealing anyone's thunder. I'm referring to the mom being praised for slapping her young son around and the news media even talking about making her woman of the year.

First let me explain my views on raising a well-balanced disciplined child. I believe corporal punishment is a supreme act of love in terms of long-term survival. Nothing instills a stronger conscious in a child than corporal punishment. A child raised with a balanced of love and discipline have by far the best chance of long-term survival.

I believe, used, as a last resort corporal punishment is a far more powerful form of love when raising the young. Many times the young will hate the one that gives them hard tough discipline. Today far too many parents see a child as a love item to be doted on, which I think is a terrible way to raise a child.

A child is a separate individual that should be taught responsibility and accountability to be a productive citizen many years later. Instead today many parents try to always please the child to make the child love them, which I think is a self-centered irresponsible parent.

The child that hated the disciplinarian most of the time years later will thank God for the only one who gave him the tools to survive. You see this intense almost spiritual like love many youngster years later will have for a hard nose strict disciplinarian sports coach. Now, back to the Mom that was slapping her kid around, God bless her.

I may disagree with her method but God bless her heart for caring and doing the best that she knew how to protect her child. I'm one that thinks a parent should never use their hands to discipline a child and especially a teenager. With parents of old that would be a complete no, no.

I believe when using corporal punishment and as a last resort one, two, three, or what amounts of licks should always be announced first. There is an old axiom that says: "A general should never give an order he knows

will not be obeyed." And by the same token I don't
think a parent should ever give a child corporal
punishment unless he/she knows it will administer a
fair amount of pain.

Otherwise, corporal punishment without pain just
breeds contempt and disrespect. Just like when a
mother tells a kid fifty times "Don't do that," to me in a
reverse way that is actually teaching disobedience. The
most important thing in child raising is consistence
then the child will know what to expect.

But, when a child is allowed to disobey fifty times and
on the fifty first time the parent is in a bad mood or
fed up and backhand's the kid off a chair, that's no
way to raise a child. Back to the kid being slapped
around, he knew not to dare resist his mom, but he
also knew he would not have to take any physical pain,
too.

The truth of the matter is her type of behavior actually
showed her lack of control over her son. A parent in
complete control would have just said, go home I will
deal with you later. And later at home she would have
put two or three hard painful licks on his ass that
would have really hurt.

I'm just glad I raised my kids over forty years ago;
otherwise today I would be in jail.
SIRMANS LOG: 02 MAY 2015, 1305 HOURS.

**IT'S A PHONY USA ECONOMY FOOL. WRITER
LETS IT ALL HANG OUT IN DEEP, DEEP ANGER.**

It is getting to where I am writing more and more

Insight On Trumpism And The Only Thing That Can Save USA From Total Doom

notes or very short one or two paragraph articles. The reason is I have mostly said it all that truly matters, and to say more is just mostly a waste of my time.

Very few want a taste of my bitter medicine. Seems my great wisdom will only be appreciated after a lot of unnecessary great pain and suffering takes place in this great country. A lot of people in the USA know we have lost our way.

They know the country is in serious trouble, and can't survive on its present course. We have a situation like the seven blind men examining an elephant. One thought the legs were tree trunks, and another thought the tail was a rope.

The USA economy and the whole inner moral and culture fabric of the country are coming apart at the seams. The conservatives bless their hearts, at least they are aware and can see the handwriting on the wall and want to stop the madness.

Whereas the liberals are too shallow to be aware of or even know the economy is in danger of totally collapsing from too much spending. The liberal are hell-bent on starving the military and social spending this great nation out of existence, period.

Sure, the conservatives are aware of the over spending danger and wants to do whatever it takes to save our country, but in my view they doesn't have the perspective to see the big picture and will wild goose chase down endless false paths.

However, this is where my great supernatural wisdom comes into play and sets me apart from all but a

Insight On Trumpism And The Only Thing That Can Save USA From Total Doom

handful. "There is always more than one way to skin a cat." And there are countless ways of saving the USA. However, I believe I am one of a handful with the deep, deep perspective to actually see the moving parts to proper dissect the USA economy.

I have the ability to see that the evil 1938 socialist minimum wage law took the discipline out of the USA economy. That caused the USA economy to be a phony weak P.... of an economy ever since that day. That almost 80 years ago fatal mistake must first be corrected before it is even possible to think about saving the great USA.

The USA must have a strong disciplined economy first before it will ever be able to save our culture, morals, or the economy itself and in that same order. This is fact, I see it, and I know it, but how many in power even know this or will agree with me on this, none is the answer.

So be it, I can shout it on the mountaintop, but I can't make anyone hear me. I love my country, and I'm mad, and I'm angry, but I know I must calm myself and continue the emergency distress call for USA survival, that is my destiny.
SIRMANS LOG: 29 APRIL 2015, 2032 HOURS.

A 2016 PRESIDENTIAL ELECTION MIND BLOWING ANALYSIS

I ,Freddie L Sirmans Sr. believe the 2016 presidential election may become so polarized that hoards of Christians, independents, conservatives, etc. like never before will turnout and vote. November 2016 may be the most important United States election since 1776 in my view. It will determine if the United States

Insight On Trumpism And The Only Thing That Can Save USA From Total Doom

survives as a free nation or survives at all, period.

I, great writer if I had any real sense I wouldn't touch this hot potato issue with a ten-foot pole, but knowing me I have no business being a writer in the first place. The Dem's and liberals knows they must win the 2016 presidential election at all cost, or the evil 1938 socialist minimum wage law may finally be repealed. "I wish, the last part I just threw that in there for my sake, y'all."

Sure, there are a lot of republican candidates going for the 2016 presidential gold, but I believe the real drama and action is going to be on the Dem's side. The reason I say this is I think the real movers and shakers on the Democratic side doesn't think Mrs. Clinton can win this milestone election.

Of course, no one over there is ever going to admit to anything of the sort. But, "you can bet your bottom dollar that ways and actions always speak louder than words." Folks, I'm a writer and could be totally wrong on this whole matter, I'm just writing what I believe.

Still, I think the long political knives are being sharpened within the Democratic Party. And before this 2016 presidential election is over a lot of Democratic political blood is going to be spilled. In 2016 for the Dem's and the sake of their power everything is on the line, even the welfare state itself, and believe me the knock out drag out is not going to be pretty, y'all.

The smart money thinks the republicans will keep control of both houses of congress in 2016. That means if the republicans win the 2016 presidency they will have a trifecta, which means the liberal and Democratic Party power monopoly starting with the

Insight On Trumpism And The Only Thing That Can Save USA From Total Doom

"New deal" may finally be broken. Hallelujah. As you can see, all of the marbles are at stake for the liberals and Dem's. Myself, I see the dawning of a new day coming, people.

This is my one man's analysis of what's so much at stake here concerning this milestone 2016 election. We'll see, just how this real life soap opera ultimately plays out. Stay tuned.
SIRMANS LOG: 23 APRIL 2015, 1438 HOURS.

JUST A FEW WORDS OF WISDOM:
Economically wise, until our cruel evil 1938 socialist minimum wage law is repealed, no matter what the conservatives or the republicans do the game is still being played on a liberalism home court.

It is no longer a matter of if the great USA will be over powered by liberalism but how soon. If our phony hog-tied economy doesn't sink us first, we are already up to our neck in a vast moral decay and culture rotted liberalism swamp and the only relief in sight is repealing our evil 1938 socialist minimum wage law. But, I seem to be the only one with the God given wisdom to see the light on this, I pound and I pound, only to thick sculls and deaf ears.

So be it, I have filled my destiny and done my duty. I will start closing by saying this: Many people have endured great pain and suffering and said "They were actually glad it happened because it opened their eyes to things right before them that they could never see before." That is what has happen to the great USA, our liberal induced welfare state has lulled almost everyone asleep, the nation will just have to experience the pain and suffering and learn the hard way if the nation survives.

Insight On Trumpism And The Only Thing That Can Save USA From Total Doom

The prevailing thinking today is government owes us a living and is responsible for the people's survival. However, nothing could be further from the real truth, it is just the opposite. The people or private enterprise is responsible for the survival of government not the other way around; government is a parasite and can't survive unless the people support it.

The USA government is taking from 40 percent of the people and using that seized profit to take care of the other 60 percent of the people. Plus, we will soon be over 20,000,000,000,000,000,000 in debt and counting. Now, if anyone thinks this can last very much longer you are a dumb ignorant fool in my view. **SIRMANS LOG: 21 APRIL 2015, 0005 HOURS.**

COLD REALITY CHECK:
Sure, anyone with an ounce of economic sense should know that the reasonable answer to the USA economy problem is to first balance the budget. But, the cold reality is the liberals have made so many voters government dependent that it is political suicide for any individual or political party to dare go there, and expect to remain in power.

It is just impossible to balance the USA budget without creating a smaller pie, which in the short run is going to cause some extra pain. And guess what, to hell with what's best down the road, what have you done for me lately is all that's going to matter in the voting booth for the masses of government dependents.

Obviously, politically no political party is ever going to be able to balance the budget to get control of the USA economy, period. However, no political party may be able to balance the budget but a true free market place economy definitely can.

Not only can a true free market place economy balance the budget, it will send liberalism packing and take our country back from all of these shallow minded do-good talking heads with weak survive instincts. The only true answer to saving the USA is not about getting lost on our phony hog-tied economy, immigration, or our insane foreign policy; it is about repealing the 1938 minimum wage law.

That will set free our hog-tied USA economy, then the economy will have the force and power to kick ass, send liberalism packing, balance the budget, and do what ever it take to save this great nation of individual freedom. Otherwise, there is not going to be a USA.

Take that as a dose of cold reality, writer, Freddie L Sirmans Sr. style. How do you like me now?
SIRMANS LOG: 10 APRIL 2015, 2228 HOURS.

Freddie L Sirmans Sr. weight losing helpful hint using the "Positive thinking" technique.
The definition of the positive thinking technique I'm talking about is: One takes a short saying or quote and repeats it over and over to ones self a minimum of fifty times or more every day.

It may take up to six months or more to start feeling strong results. This is the quote I use: "I can keep my body slim and healthy through God which strengthens me." Just leave God off or substitute another deity if one doesn't believe in God.

Insight On Trumpism And The Only Thing That Can Save USA From Total Doom

Lets face it folks, some of us like me are compulsive over eaters; I have suffered with this disorder ever since I was a child. Some of us just simply can't do it alone, that is why turning to God by saying through God which strengthens me is all-powerful.

However, it doesn't work over night, it takes a while to break through to the subconscious. But, if one stays the course long enough positive results will be realized.

Salt and sodium are the biggest factors in controlling high blood pressure. I buy the gallon jugs of drinking water with 0 sodium. Also, I buy the little squeeze bottles of fresh lemon juice and drink lemon water as my main beverage, no sugar added for me. I believe some water is loaded with sodium for the same reason as processed foods, be aware.

NOTE:
There is a simple universal fact about life and survival, risk and struggle is a greater part of it. If too much risk and struggle is taken out of life, then its purpose and value greatly diminishes. It is in our DNA from evolving over the eons. Repealing our evil 1938 socialist minimum wage law will rescue the USA from our dying liberal welfare state, which has made the USA a P.... of a society.

LIBERAL SUICIDE SPENDING
This is a subject I decided to revisit. There is a conservative faction that wants to bring about a states convention to demand the government balance it's annul budget.

Insight On Trumpism And The Only Thing That Can Save USA From Total Doom

On the surface having a convention to do that sounds reasonable and maybe ought to take place. Twenty years ago I probably would have jumped on the bandwagon. However, I have evolved and now realize liberalism has no boundaries or limits to what it will go to keep over spending.

Today I think any convention of the sort would more than likely cause a total disaster. The first reason is it wouldn't solve the problem. Our welfare state beast is ignoring the constitution and the law now and just adding new laws are not going to make this beast change its ways. The next reason involves human nature.

Liberals tends to be far more intelligent and smarter than conservatives but as a rule are shallow surface dwelling thinkers. The conservative's advantage has always been their focused staying power and deep sound judgment. However, there is a world of difference between today's conservatives and those in the founding fathers days.

Ever since the "New deal" and the come about of our welfare state conservatives has become almost as moral corrupted and shallow minded as liberals. It is a waste of time to pass more laws trying to force liberals to control spending.

They have weak survival instincts and respects no threats in spending from here to kingdom come. But, never forget liberals are not dumb or stupid, when giving up any of their own money they are the stingiest of any group. What it actually boils down to is they struggle with not being selfish to a fault, and that includes spending other people money.

Insight On Trumpism And The Only Thing That Can Save USA From Total Doom

Most conservatives are self-bound by morals and emotional boundaries such as guilt, shame, etc. Where as liberals tends to be far less restricted when going after something they truly want. Nothing that is within the law is going deter a liberal lion/lionness from grabbing power and keeping it.

Power is what this liberal suicide spending is all about. Social spending keeps liberals in power and no amount of morals; love of the country, or anything legal is going to stand in their way of holding on to power. Many liberals tend to be aimless but you give a liberal a cause or a goal and you got an almost unstoppable force on your hand.

If the great USA is to ever get control over suicide over spending from the liberals it can only be done with a physical barrier. So, here we go again, that means repealing the 1938 minimum wage law. Enacting that law is what took away a government-spending barrier in the first place.

That law gave liberals absolute power over private enterprise and private property rights and enable them to tax spend inflate, tax spend inflate, tax spend inflate in a never-ending upward spiral. In fact I don't believe its possible for any free nation to remain free very long with liberalism and liberals at the helm.

Freedom and democracy demands a responsible and self-controlled populace to last over a hundred years in my view. The liberals seized complete control over USA private business enterprise and private property rights with the enacting of the 1938 minimum wage law.

Insight On Trumpism And The Only Thing That Can Save USA From Total Doom

Unless that law is repealed this nation will never remain free to 2038 let alone more than a hundred years since the law was enacted.
SIRMANS LOG: 02 APRIL 2015, 2107 HOURS.

CAN THE USA ECONOMY AVOID TOTAL CHAOS IF THE ECONOMY COLLAPSES

I felt like doing some thinking out loud on paper on how much time the country have before our economy totally collapses. I will try to make this article short and not get carried away.

I will start by saying anyone with an ounce of economic wisdom should know that this madness can't possibly be sustained. No one knows how or when all of this economic madness is going to finally play out in the end, not even me.

But, I do know two things our welfare state is about to butt heads on. Number one is the days of our welfare state in the role of social and family provider is over, the government just doesn't realize it yet.

The other thing is our welfare state beast will never surrender it power of being a social and family provider even if it means giving up our sovereignty, selling off the country, or whatever to hold on that role.

It is a role the government should never have been in from the start. Government in the role of super provider is like feeding on itself or eating its young. Nature's law of taking the course of least resistance can be extremely disarming and seductive.

Insight On Trumpism And The Only Thing That Can Save USA From Total Doom

That is because no caring and reasonable person wants to see suffering and hardship. But, like drugs, sex, gambling, and anything that gives relief and pleasure, too much of a good thing can be a trap.

While good men and women stood by the shallow minded liberals with good intent eased the government into a permanent role of being a social and family provider. This is a role that for over 6,000 years had always been with the nuclear and extended family head of household.

I'm sure over the centuries governments had tried playing daddy before but before it had always failed. And the only reason it hasn't failed so far in the USA is because of our evil 1938 socialist minimum wage law. That evil law is what has kept this farce going this long.

The evil 1938 minimum wage law has allowed the liberals to grow government unabated by inflating our currency to no end. And they call it growing the economy, which it is not; it is sheer madness and insanity in my view. Sure, this insanity can work for around four generations then it's going to be hell to pay.

That is because ever since this insanity started around 80 years ago it has rotted away the tools and foundation that allows for an organize society to exist. The tools I am referring to are a strong nuclear and extended family system, and an adequate supply of small farmers and home gardeners. That would provide some emergency backup bartering capacity to buy

Insight On Trumpism And The Only Thing That Can Save USA From Total Doom

time in case the economy collapses and money was worthless.

In term of long-term survival nothing can take the place of the strong nuclear and extended family system. Without the strong nuclear family system not enough men and women of sound judgment can be produced to maintain an orderly responsible society.

Only the strong nuclear family will make sure proper norms and traditions are instilled in the very young. Experienced wisdom, good morals, and spiritual values must be instilled and passed on or chaos will eventually result.

Sure, living in a world of plenty with full stomachs most of us are so caring with good intentions that we never wake up to smell the coffee. But, I'm here to tell you that we Americans along with much of the industrialized world below the surface are spoiled rotten.

We are comfortable and living in a dream, not knowing that we have almost no tools to survive on when this mad insane economy soon collapses. Without the umbrella of a strong nuclear and extended family system very few are going to make great self-sacrifices for greedy selfish thankless strangers. And self-sacrificing is what it will take to survive as a nation during severe hard and tough times.

However, all of this coming doom can be avoided by repealing the evil 1938 socialist minimum wage law. Even repealing the 1938 minimum wage law is going to cause much pain and hardship but it will be controllable and not turn into chaos.

Insight On Trumpism And The Only Thing That Can Save USA From Total Doom

Once the USA economy is free and unshackled it won't take much to eat and survive, and there is nothing more powerful on earth than a genuine true free market economy. There is no doubt in my mind it will save the USA and western civilization. And may the Gods smile down on this great nation.

P.S. A non minimum wage genuine true free market place economy won't allow inflation and a phony currency for very long, like a liquid a true free market place economy will soon seek its own level.
SIRMANS LOG: 29 MARCH 2015, 0101 HOURS.

THE WORLD WOULD BE A COLD DREARY PLACE WITHOUT LIBERALISM

I'm going to briefly say a few words on liberalism. Sure, I criticize liberalism as much as anyone but I love liberals as well as all people. The world would be a cold dreary existence without liberals and liberalism, who else would guarantee that Bamba is safe and the soft emotional side of life prevails.

However, there has never been and never will be a society that survives very long with liberalism at the helm. The evil 1938 socialist minimum wage law allowed liberalism to gain control of the USA government. And ever since layer by layer they have been running this great USA ship of state aground.

Liberals have a weak survival instinct and can't see any danger in spending this nation out of existence. They have no concept of the pain, suffering, and turmoil that will result from a collapsed economy due to reckless spending. Plus, on the other hand the

Insight On Trumpism And The Only Thing That Can Save USA From Total Doom

liberals have made far too many people government dependent for Republicans to succeed in trying to balance the USA budget.

That approach will surly fail for two main reasons; the first reason is it will definitely create a smaller economy pie, which in the short run will make the economy worse. The second reason is the liberal media and general public is economically ignorant and living in the now and could care less about what is best down the road.

So, when the pie starts getting smaller and painful the Republicans will be booted out of office short order. I think the republicans should just tread water until after November 2016, then do the deed I have been advocating.

Now, I will say again what I have said a thousand times or more, if the republican wants to save this great nation, repeal the evil 1938 socialist minimum wage law, period. That will set free our shackled free market place economy. And there is nothing on earth more powerful than a genuine true free market place economy.

If the republicans set our economy free all they will need to do is be still, the true free economy will take it from there and save this great nation for our children and grand children. However, I'm a realist, I know anything I say, just the opposite will be done, so be it.

In my view there is nothing innate about being a liberal, that is why before our welfare state it was almost unheard of to find a poor liberal. Before our welfare state our poor always had the strongest

morals, they could be trusted to work in ones home
and very few would take an unborn life.

Today, one poor minority group in the USA are killing
the unborn at a higher rate than anywhere in the
world. The fact is if any nation is to survive long term
Liberalism must never be allowed to completely
takeover.

However, there is no denying it; ever since the "New
deal" and the 1938 minimum wage law liberalism has
dominated the USA government, period. Liberalism,
some of it is in the stars but environment always over
rules that, which is why I am totally convinced that
only repealing the 1938 minimum wage law can break
the liberalism death choke hold on this nation.

Liberalism at our helm is like having a kid behind the
wheel. Plus, our liberal welfare state has destroyed our
culture and morals, but the most deadly of all, it has
destroyed our sense of sound judgment. Survival then
becomes a far more risky business, sort of like the roll
of the dice, or not even dealing with a full deck.
SIRMANS LOG: 26 MARCH 2015, 1414 HOURS.

**THE FOLLY OF THINKING THE USA BUDGET CAN
BE BALANCED???**
A genuine true non-phony free market place economy
without exception must be able to set its own wages
and prices, period. The liberals in charge of the
government seized that right when they enacted the
evil 1938 socialist minimum wage law.

That act castrated the USA economy and has led to the
destruction of our culture and morals. And until the
USA economy is given back its power by repealing the

Insight On Trumpism And The Only Thing That Can Save USA From Total Doom

evil 1938 socialist minimum wage law nothing can break the liberals choke hold on this great nation. Otherwise, there is simply no way this great nation of individual freedom can ever be saved.

Men and women of sound mind with strong survival instincts must give the USA economy back its true power, that way it can save this great nation. Nothing else has the power and discipline to drain this vast liberal swamp and prevent individual freedom from disappearing off the face of the earth forever. God save the USA the last bastion of true individual freedom left in the world today.

The truth of the matter is government is actually a parasite; it can only survive if it has a host to take from. Government is not part of the economy but what it does greatly affects the economy. Every society must have a means of protecting itself from internal and external threats and dangers, and that makes having some form of government a must.

Most governments have the power to take over that is why most private sector host has strong built in protections and total control over the money supply. But, like they say, "The way to hell is paved with good intentions."

On the surface the government doing good and helping people doesn't seem like a threat, and it is not in perspective on a temporary basis. But, in reality government must never become a social and family provider more than on a temporary basis if a free nation is to survive long term.

Whoever is the provider is the boss like it or not. That is why in the USA and Western Europe for all practical

Insight On Trumpism And The Only Thing That Can Save USA From Total Doom

purpose the welfare state has taken over. Today there are far too many people dependent on the government to ever put government spending on a diet.

In Western Europe and now in the USA the money priority first goes to the welfare state over the military and all else. And there is only contempt for the profit driven private business enterprise host. Plus, private business days may be numbers because liberal media and the masses don't understand profit and hate it.

Still, there is a savior waiting on a white horse ready to ride in to rescue western civilization. But first, the evil 1938 socialist minimum law must be shot with a silver bullet or a stake driven through its heart by repealing or getting rid of all minimum wage laws entirely. This evil poison pill law must be buried to never rise again for any democracy to ever be safe.

In terms of raw bare boned survival using good intentions and doing the right thing may cause Mother Nature to spit in your face. Just look at the animal kingdom with raw nature, there is no place for good intentions or doing the right thing, except to starve.

Now, you look at the USA economic situation, from a political point of view good intentions and doing the right thing I believe will surely get you booted out of power, period. Folks, let me stop right here and explain, I'm a writer and I write it as I see it. I can be wrong, in fact I hope I am wrong on some of the dire things I see coming down the pike.

I have said it before and am going to say it again, anyone that still thinks the USA and western Europe can be saved as welfare states is economically ignorant in my view. Maybe I'm the one who is ignorant.

Insight On Trumpism And The Only Thing That Can Save USA From Total Doom

However, I believe I can dissect and understand the inner workings of an economy as well as anyone.

Yet, for the life of me I can't see any social and family provider welfare state doing anything but slowly devouring its own survival host, which is private business enterprise. Economically, it is just impossible for a welfare state to survive very much longer by constantly dwindling its own only survival host, which is profit driven private business enterprise.

Government can take only so much profit before there is none left to take. Anyone with common sense should know that the USA can't forever reckless spend and keep going deeper and deeper into debt. A reasonable person should conclude that the right thing to do is balance the budget and get your physical house in order.

Sure, that is the responsible thing to do if you are talking about around 80 years ago right after the minimum wage law was enacted. But, today for a political party to take that type of normal responsible action is political suicide.

Now, here is where my super wisdom comes into play. OK, lets just imagine that at the snap of fingers all of the USA debts are paid free and clear, do you think the health of the nation would be solved? My answer would be no! Our debt is a currency problem but civilization existed long before a currency was invented.

The main problems with the USA and western civilization are culture and moral in my view. Contrary to the common view I believe in free nations the economy is the real disciplinarian that actually guards and protects the nations culture and morals.

Insight On Trumpism And The Only Thing That Can Save USA From Total Doom

Sure, we are a nation ruled by law not by man, but I believe the economy is the real power that pulls the strings behind the scene. Also, I believe liberalism is actually what's destroying the USA, which could never have happen with a genuine true free market place economy.

I feel the economy the USA has today is a phony P.... of an economy and has been that way ever since the evil 1938 minimum wage law was enacted. The economy the USA has today doesn't have the power or discipline to protect itself or the nation's culture and morals.

Once the 1938 minimum wage law was enacted, that allowed liberalism a foot in the door to inflate the currency and grow government to no end. Since then the minimum wage law gave government absolute power over prices and wages. Once that happened the aggressive liberals has played to the basic weaknesses in our human nature by promising the moon and back.

The minimum wage law gave government complete control over private property rights and private business enterprise, which it had never had before in the history of the country. By repealing the minimum wage law the economy would regain its power to guard and protect the nations culture and morals, plus boom the economy in real growth not any phony inflated growth like today.

So, the republican think they can take on our welfare state beast and balance the budget, plus remain in power. Well, I'm one that thinks they are in for a very rude awakening. I hope I'm wrong, but I think the

Insight On Trumpism And The Only Thing That Can Save USA From Total Doom

beast will defend itself and win. I truly feel only a genuine true free market place economy minus any minimum wage law has the power and ability to take down this beast.

They will never agree with me, but I feel the only wise course the republicans has left to save the USA is to repeal the evil 1938 socialist minimum wage law, "That is all she wrote." As to liberals saving the country, they are the ones hell bent on destroying it and too shallow to even realize it.

SIRMANS LOG: 17 MARCH 2015, 1748 HOURS.

IS THE USA ENTERING A TOTAL BREAKDOWN OF ITS SOCIETY?

You can't get blood out of a turnip. And you can't have a peaceful and orderly society without strong discipline. So, in my view the USA is entering a totally break down of our p.... of a society.

In authoritarian societies brute muscle power and force can be used to maintain discipline. Whereas in free societies people have individual rights and laws that must be obeyed to maintain strong discipline. But, in a free society when there is no brute power and force to maintain discipline two things is a must to prevent a total breakdown of that society.

Those two must things are first a genuine true free market place economy and second a strong nuclear and extended family system. A nations economy trumps everything because everyone must have food and warmth to survive. That is the reason immigration is out of control our welfare state allows our poor and uneducated to avoid doing hot hard work to keep the nation fed.

Insight On Trumpism And The Only Thing That Can Save USA From Total Doom

Somebody gotta do that type work or we all will starve. Now, you try to convince a farmer with his harvest rotting in the field that I'm wrong. Next is the nuclear family, there never has and never will be a society that last very long without a strong nuclear and extended family system.

It is almost impossible to maintain an orderly and peaceful society without making sure the very young are taught proper norms and traditions. That is what happen to the black community, the black man right out of slavery enforced and maintained discipline in the home.

He made sure proper norms and traditions were instilled in the very young before he was kicked out of the home by the welfare state. The welfare state never concerned itself with proper behavior and to this day is still financing its destruction.

Many people are worried about the government completely taking over, well, with the way things are falling apart, the day may come when the people rise up and demand the government take over.
SIRMANS LOG: 12 MARCH 2015, 2229 HOURS.

ABOUT THIS NET NEUTRALITY TROJAN HORSE GIFT
I, great writer Freddie L Sirmans Sr. decided to briefly comment on this "Net Neutrality" thing. The fact is I haven't read hardly anything or listen to very much about it on radio or TV. Still, I decided to weigh in on it anyway.

Insight On Trumpism And The Only Thing That Can Save USA From Total Doom

The truth is what they do don't bother me much one-way or the other. In many ways I feel the world would be better off if the Internet would never have been invented, but its here and anyone standing in the way of progress will get ran over.

I don't need details because I know once the government gets its greed little tax grubbing hands on the throat of the Internet it is ruined forever. It will end up just like our ruined health care system, and screwed up with very few able to afford it.

Before the government seized control of our USA health care system the poor and middle class could pay out of pocket their doctor visits and not over run the nations emergency rooms. Right now, most people don't need the Internet to survive, and the vast majority goes about their daily lives without it. But, once the government seizes enough control over it all of that is going to come to screeching halt.

Our welfare state beast is already slobbering and licking its chops seeing the Internet as a cash cow. They are going to make it where you can't get any kind of health care, a job, or anything else without going on line.

Right now the problem is no one knows how the Internet is going to be taxed, but I assure you the Internet will be made where you can't survive without it or paying to use it.

Warning, I'm fixing to go on a rant and it is my one-man belief and opinion, nothing more. Cease now, or continue reading at your own risk. So, if you want to know what I really think about our future, I may be wrong, but I think the USA will be fortunate if it survive 2015 without a totally economic collapse. And if we survive 2015 this economic lying and insanity can't possibly last much longer.

Insight On Trumpism And The Only Thing That Can Save USA From Total Doom

This is cold hard reality stuff, I just hope they don't start banning or burning my books. I believe that almost everything the USA government puts out concerning our current phony p.... of an economy is propaganda, period. I know beyond a shadow of a doubt that only repealing our evil 1938 socialist minimum wage law entirely can save the USA at this late stage.

Sure, I'm going to be dismissed as a nut case or kook and ignored for now. But, hate me; disagree with me or whatever, I know with my great supernatural wisdom history will prove me right without a doubt. Praise be to God. All of this economic insanity and madness is about to come to a head in my view.

I believe there is an energy or force governing the universe, you can call it God, a superior being, mother nature, natural selection, destiny, or whatever, but it maintains a balance in the universe and prevents total disorder.

Every action has a reaction counter part, every positive has a negative counter part, and every good has an evil counter part and vice-versa. Only balance maintains order in the universe. And it affects everything that exists, it is sort of like the whole universe is a unit of one. It is like good and evil is two sides of the same coin.

I will close with this, if you really want to understand and know how an economy and free market place is suppose to work read Freddie L Sirmans Sr. books if you can take it.

It saddens me to say this but western civilization has almost become a modern day Sodom and Gomorrah. So, guess what, the universe is beginning to adjust and balance all this same sex marring and mass

Insight On Trumpism And The Only Thing That Can Save USA From Total Doom

murdering in the womb with??? You figure it out!!! I know but I will remain mute.

All human emotions evolved to aid human survival in some way. The negative emotions such as evil, hate, etc. are primarily geared to destroy in some way. So, in the eyes of nature there is no such thing as a good or bad emotion they are all just tools in maintaining a balance to keep order in the universe.

I believe when you see evil, evil seemingly like everywhere it is to counter balance something parading as good that is as equal threatening to human survival. My guess is evil is being balanced against the threats to procreation to aid human survival in some way. The process of procreation is in grave danger in the USA and western civilization and Mother Nature is stepping in.

In the USA and Western Europe there is mass means of birth control on demand, mass abortions and killing in the womb on demand, and now we are on a fast path to mass same sex marriages on demand. Now, if you don't think that is a moral and grave threat to procreation and the survival of our species, you are an ignorant fool with a weak survival instinct. Yet, you are the norm, this is what the liberal induced welfare state has brought us to.

Again, disagree if you will, I'm warning you, only removing or repealing the evil socialist minimum wage laws entirely from the USA and western economies can save western civilization from total doom. That is the only thing that can drain this vast liberal swamp. There are just too many two-faced anti-survival monsters dwelling in this self-gratification do-good-er swamp to contend with, the S.O.B. must be drained if the USA is to survive, period.

SIRMANS LOG: 24 FEBRUARY 2015, 1738 HOURS.

Insight On Trumpism And The Only Thing That
Can Save USA From Total Doom

**BOOK #2 ENJOY THIS NICE LITTLE FABLE
WRITTEN BY FREDDIE L SIRMANS SR.**

Chapter 1
Once upon a time there was a
little town called Health-land kingdom,
located right off the big super MD
highway leading to the great cure-all
metropolis. In this town lived
vitamins, minerals,   herbs, humans,
and other nutrients.

The town's main goal was to
keep all of its citizens healthy
because anyone that   they failed to
keep healthy would have to face
terrible traffic jams on the super MD
highway leading to the great cure-all
metropolis.

Jim-Niacin (vitamin B-3). Jim-
Niacin doesn't stand alone; he is a
member of the very powerful B
vitamin family. In Health-land Jim-
Niacin's job is essential to promote
life and good health. He regulates
the metabolism and assists in other
body processes, even though he is
needed in small amounts compared
to proteins and carbohydrates.
As a coenzyme Jim-Niacin works
to make sure the human body
functions as it should. There are two
major types of vitamins: the water
soluble and the oil soluble. Jim-Niacin belongs to the
water-soluble type vitamins, therefore his doses
must be replaced everyday because
the human body doesn't store his

Insight On Trumpism And The Only Thing That Can Save USA From Total Doom

doses like the oil soluble type.

Since Jim-Niacin is only one
member of the very powerful B
vitamin family he shouldn't work
alone; he should be balanced with
other B vitamin members. Jim-Niacin
is not a bad or evil fellow, but he does
have a bad reputation.

Humans are afraid of Jim-Niacin
and rightly so because in too high
doses he may damage the liver, or in
too low doses he does no good. But,
that is not the only reason human
fear Jim-Niacin. Jim-Niacin deals with
circulation and the skin, and he will
heat the skin up like it is on fire and
turn it as red as a beet.
When this happens to a human
for the first time, it will scare some
humans half to death, but don't be put
off, the flushing of the skin is normal
when dealing with Jim-Niacin. It's not
pretty or pleasant but that is how Jim-
Niacin unclogs the capillaries and
small blood vessels throughout the
body.

Captain Fredrico (human). Orry
Fredrico is one of many humans that
Was born and raised in Health-land
Kingdom. Orry Fredrico is a
Carpenter by trade, but as long as he
Could remember he loved the sea.
As a small child he would stand by
The ocean for hours just staring out to
Sea.
      As a teenager he would try to

Insight On Trumpism And The Only Thing That Can Save USA From Total Doom

Hop aboard any boat going salt water
Fishing. During his senior year in high
School he went on one of those deep
Sea fishing cruises that goes out for
Four or five hours at a time. On this
Cruises he met Jan Flemmings. Jan
Also loved the sea and they instantly
Became attracted to each other.
Within days Jim started dating Jan.

VC (vitamin C). VC also belongs
To the water-soluble type of vitamin.
VC   is truly a heavyweight among
Vitamins. VC is known as a very
Power antioxidant. He is a mighty
Human body protector. He protects
the human body against harmful
effects of pollution.   He helps to
prevent cancer.   He helps to lower
cholesterol and other protection
functions.

Scurvy is a disease that moves
in when there is a deficiency in
vitamin C protection. Years ago,
passengers on ships on long voyages
without fresh fruits and vegetables
had a problem dealing with scurvy.

Jan Flemmings (human). Jan
is a Health-land Kingdom toy
soldier's brat. Just like Captain
Fredrico she has always loved the
sea. She was mostly unanchored
until she met her   soul mate Orry
Fredrico. At first she thought he
loved the sea too much and would not
be a good provider, but his dreamy

84

Insight On Trumpism And The Only Thing That Can Save USA From Total Doom

bedroom eyes soon won her over.

VE (vitamin E). VE belongs to the oil soluble type of vitamin. VE is another mighty antioxidant. VE is very important in fighting cancer and cardiovascular disease. Vitamin E is a giant in so many ways. VE is a natural blood thinner. He promotes good blood circulation, he promotes healthy skin, healthy hair, and so many other healthy body functions. Vitamin E actually belongs to a family of eight but falls into two major groups. These two groups are tocopherols and tocotrienols. It is the alpha-tocopherols form that is the most potent. That is the group VE belongs to.

John-Pyridoxine (vitamin B-6). John-Pyridoxine like his cousin Jim-Niacin is a member of the very powerful B vitamin family. The fact is John-Pyridoxine is involved in more bodily functions than any other single nutrient. John-Pyridoxine deals with both the mental and physical health.

He deals with water retention, sodium and potassium balance, and fights hard against allergies, arthritis, asthma, carpal tunnel syndrome, and on and on. Just like his cousin Jim-Niacin, John-Pyridoxine shouldn't fight alone; he should be balanced with other members of the mighty B vitamin family.

Insight On Trumpism And The Only Thing That Can Save USA From Total Doom

Mister Disease. Mister and his family   showed up one day in Health-land Kingdom. No one seems to know where he came from. All anyone knows is he is mean and evil. He has no friends and is known to attack humans sometimes without provocation.

He has no conscience and will attack anyone that is weak and helpless. The town and kingdom has tried to keep him out, but somehow he always sneaks back in. Our vitamins, minerals, herbs and others nutrient citizens have done a good job fighting him off, but Mister Disease is a very, very tough customer.

Jim-Niacin and the other nutrient protectors of Health-land Kingdom were joyfully patting themselves on the back because they were doing a good job protecting the city's population from Mister Disease and his cohorts. Jim-Niacin decided to telephone his cousin John-Pyridoxine. Jim could hear the phone making its fourth ring.

"Hello," said John-Pyridoxine.
" This is Jim-Niacin, I decided to give you a call and touch base on a matter that I've been tossing around in my mind lately."
"Tell me about it," said John-Pyridoxine.

Insight On Trumpism And The Only Thing That Can Save USA From Total Doom

"Well, I've been thinking that all
of the vitamins, minerals, humans,
herbs, and other nutrient citizens
should get together and have a big
town hall meeting. What do you
think."

"I think it is a very good idea,"
said john-Pyridoxine.
" Good, then it's a go, I'm going
to start right away making plans,"
said Jim-Niacin. "John you take care
now, I'll talk to you later."
" Bye," said John-Pyridoxine.

Chapter 2
Orry Fredrico and Jan
Flemmings got married after a one
year engagement. Orry got an
associate degree in carpentry from
the local technical college. Twenty
five years later Orry and Jan are now
the parents of a seventeen-year-old
son Rob, and a fifteen-year-old
daughter Melinda.

Almost everyone calls Orry   by
his nickname Captain Fredrico after
he bought his first boat about fifteen
years ago. The boat was a fourteen
footer with a big Mercury motor.
Captain Fredrico now operates his
own contracting business.

It is almost six o'clock p.m. when
Captain Fredrico lets himself in the
carport door which opens directly into
the kitchen. He found his wife Jan

Insight On Trumpism And The Only Thing That Can Save USA From Total Doom

bending over checking her meat loaf
in the oven.

"Hello dear," said Captain
Fredrico in a somewhat tired voice.
" Hello Orry, how did your day
" Pretty good, but my right wrist
that's been bothering me the last
couple of weeks seems to be getting
worse, especially at night after I fall
asleep.   Sometimes I wake up with a
numb tingling in my right hand. It
feels like somebody is sticking pins in
my hands."

"Orry, I think you need to check
with one of the vitamin citizens. That
sounds like something John-
pyridoxine might be able to help you
with."

"I think you are right dear, I will
give him a call in a few days.

After Marrying Orry, Jan Fredrico
decided to postpone a career of her
own. Becoming a full time housewife
and mother was very fulfilling to Jan.
She even took on the   awesome job
of home schooling her kids.

VC (vitamin c) enjoys his job in
Health-land Kingdom taking care of
its citizens. He has a very good
reputation. Humans were using him
probably more than any other vitamin.
Being one of the most powerful
antioxidants, he was in great demand

Insight On Trumpism And The Only Thing That Can Save USA From Total Doom

these days.

In fact, he was being used to
fortify many of today's foods. He
thought the town hall meeting was a
great idea. Why didn't he think of it?
The vitamins and other nutrients were
doing a good job fighting off Mister
Disease, but he knew that they
couldn't let their guards down, ever.

Just like VC, VE (vitamin E) is
another very powerful antioxidant but
of the oil soluble type. VE is probably
in even greater demand these days
than VC. With so many humans
becoming diabetics these days, VE
with his natural blood thinning power
is a real workhorse. VE is also
looking forward to the big town hall
meeting coming up soon.

On this Monday morning John-
Pyridoxine was kicking back at his
office when the phone ring.
" Hello," said John-Pyridoxine.
" May I speak to John-
Pyridoxine?" said the voice on the
line.

"This is he," said John-Pyridoxine.
" I'm Captain Fredrico and I've
been told you may be able to help me
concerning an ailment. I believe I
have a case of carpal tunnel
syndrome."

"You have the right vitamin,

Insight On Trumpism And The Only Thing That Can Save USA From Total Doom

that is one of my many areas of
expertise."
" Then you will be able to help
me," said Captain Fredrico.

"Hold on a minute, I didn't say
that. Let me explain the situation
here, then I can tell you what I may
be able to do. Listen Captain, I'm
going to explain what I do, and it
should take care of your problem, but
then it may not. If I can't cure it, then
I recommend you take the super
MD highway to the cure all
metropolis."

"I understand," said Captain
Fredrico.
" Now, first off," said John-
Pyridoxine, "my maximum dose is
300 mg. per day, that way I will not
damage any nerves. In most cases
100 mg. of my dose will cure the
problem. The golden rule with taking
any nutrients is don't take more than
the recommended dose, because too
much of anything may cause
damage, and never take nutrients on
an empty stomach. So, Captain if
you understood everything I said,
come by as soon as possible. We
have a walk in policy."

"Thank you sir, I should be there
within the hour."

Mister Disease is very upset with
himself for being unable to do more
damage in Health-land Kingdom. He

Insight On Trumpism And The Only Thing That Can Save USA From Total Doom

feels he should be able to bring in
more of his friends like cancer, AIDS,
and even some of his very old friends
like the black plague.

He was getting fed up with those
damn vitamins, minerals, herbs, and
other nutrients. The thing about
those nutrients is they are keeping
him from getting a foothold in Health-
land Kingdom. He feels that if he
could just get a foothold he would be
able to start an epidemic.

Mister Disease decided that he
would just have to work harder.
Sooner or later those humans are
going to think that they are safe and
slack up on utilizing the nutrients.
That is the time he plans to throw his
best punch. He feels that if his friend
AIDS just keeps up the pressure, he
has the best shot at causing an
epidemic.

Most humans don't know Jim-
Niacin and many of those that do
tend to fear and avoid him. As one of
the smallest members of the powerful
B vitamin family, being unknown is
about to change. The reason is Jim-
Niacin along with his cousin John-
Pyridoxine are the ones that called
for and organized the town hall
meeting coming up in a few weeks.
The whole thing was originally
Jim-Niacin's idea.

Since then Jim has

invited the town fathers and secured
all of the permits needed to stage
such an event. Jim has contacted
other town nutrients and humans,
many of them had never heard of
him, or knew who he was.

Chapter 3
Captain Fredrico had lived in
Health-land Kingdom all of his life and
he loved this town. Captain Fredrico
got an invitation from Jim-Niacin to
attend the town hall meeting coming
up in a few weeks.

Captain Fredrico had heard the
name Jim-Niacin before and even
knew he was a member of the mighty
B vitamin family, but that was about
all he knew about Jim-Niacin. He
didn't know what kind of work or
anything else Jim-Niacin did.

Captain Fredrico had heard that
the vitamins and other nutrients
citizens had become concerned about
the health of Health-land Kingdom.
The main work our nutrient citizens
do is protect our human population
from characters like Mister Disease
and his friends.

The nutrients knew that cancer
and AIDS had almost destroyed a few
other towns in the Kingdom. The
town hall meeting got Captain
Fredrico to thinking. The mayoral
election will be coming up in about a
year. Captain Fredrico decided that

Insight On Trumpism And The Only Thing That Can Save USA From Total Doom

he was going to throw his hat in the
ring. Of course he would have to talk
it over with his wife Jan first.

After putting in a hard day's
work, on his drive home Captain
Fredrico thought about the pesky dry
skin that had been plaguing him for
years. It has slowly become more
and more of a problem as time past.

Now it has become a real nuisance.
It has come to the point that he has
to lotion down almost his whole body
every time he takes a shower.
He feels that is unmanly, only
women like to lotion their bodies. He
has tried everything, but to no avail.

He had even got on the crowded
super MD highway and went to the
cure all metropolis, but still to no
avail. At the cure all metropolis all
they did was to prescribe an
extremely expensive body cream that
did little better than over the counter
creams.

He felt truly at his wits end.
There didn't seem to be any hope, he
would just have to accept his
miserable fate. As Captain Fredrico
let himself in the carport door, Jan
was making a salad.
" Hello, dear," said the Captain in
a husky sexy voice.

"Hello, sweetheart," said Jan in
a wooing voice as she dropped
everything and rushed over and

Insight On Trumpism And The Only Thing That Can Save USA From Total Doom

planted a seductive kiss on her
husband's left cheek.

"Now, you go ahead and clean
up, dinner will be ready in a few
minutes. By the way Rob complained
about a bout of indigestion after
lunch."

"Did you check with Mr. Blue
Page?" said the Captain.
" Yes, he gave me the names of
several nutrients that work in that
area. The two nutrients that I decided
to use were Stewart-Ginger Root and
Henry-Acidolphilus. Each one of
them gave me heavy doses to give
Rob as needed."

"Good, now let me go ahead
and wash up, then you can tell me all
about it later." After the Captain and
all of the family had sat down to
dinner and the blessing was said, the
Captain revisited the subject of Rob's
indigestion.

"How is your stomach feeling
now, Rob," said the Captain.
" It's fine now, dad, since Mom
had a couple of the nutrients treat it."
" I wasn't sure what to do until
after my talk with Mr. Blue Page,"
said Jan.

"Mr. Blue Page gave me the
names of several nutrients that work
in the area of indigestion. These are
the names that Mr. Blue Page gave
me that deal with indigestion:

Insight On Trumpism And The Only Thing That Can Save USA From Total Doom

Stewart-Ginger Root, Calvin-
Fenugreek, Bonnie-Papaya, Henry-
Acidophilus, and Sammy-Oat bran
tablets.

He also stressed that they did
their work with either tablets or
capsules."

"Excuse me for changing the
subject, I have a very important
announcement to make," said the
captain.

"Jan, the mayoral election is
coming up in about a year and I
would like to know if you have any
objections to me throwing my hat into
the ring."

"Gee, I don't know? I've never
thought about being a politician's wife.
Do you think you can win?"
"Dad, I love it, I think it is a great
idea," said Melinda.
"Me too," said Rob.

"I can't guarantee you I will win,
but I believe if I get out there and
shake enough hands I'll have a very
good shot."
" Dad, I'll campaign for you," said
Melinda.

"Honey, If you really want to
run, then count me in as your number
one supporter," said Jan.
"Then it's all settled You are
looking at the next mayor of Health-
land Kingdom."

Insight On Trumpism And The Only Thing That Can Save USA From Total Doom

Ever since John-Pyridoxine had agreed to help his cousin Jim-Niacin organize the big town hall meeting coming up soon, he had stayed busy calling and talking to the citizens of Health-land Kingdom.

Chapter 4

Mr. Disease was aware of the big town hall meeting coming up in a few days, and he definitely was not pleased about what he was hearing. The word was they were going to try to get rid of him. Mr. Disease was not going to let that deter him, that had been tried before with his ancestors all throughout history.

Sure, the discovery of DDT, penicillin, and modern antibiotics had given his family some big setbacks, but some of his old friends like tuberculosis were beginning to make a comeback, and the new kid on the block, AIDS, was really beginning to raise hell.

Mr. Disease felt that as far as he was concerned, let them have all of the town hall meetings they want to, it was not going to put him out of business.

Mr. Disease watches the super MD highway often and as far as he could tell it was becoming even more crowded each day. Even at the big super cure all metropolis they

Insight On Trumpism And The Only Thing That Can Save USA From Total Doom

haven't been able to get rid of his
best friend Mr. Cancer. Mr. Cancer is
still doing an awful lot of damage.

On this Monday morning Jan
Fredrico   sure didn't want to battle
the traffic jams on the super MD
highway going to the cure all
metropolis. It was just one of those
days, Her daughter was down with a
cold and she herself was dealing with
a slight kidney infection.

She didn't know? Maybe it was
something she ate that was causing
her back a slight ache in the area of
her kidney. She knew that it would
save her a lot of money and time if
she called Mr. Blue Page and found
out which vitamins, minerals, herbs,
or other nutrients that specialized in
the areas of their ailments.

Jan decided to give the nutrients
twenty-four hours to do their work,
then if there was no obvious
improvement she would get on the
crowded super MD highway to the
cure all metropolis. Jan dialed Mr.
Blue Page. The voice on the line said, " You have
reached Mr. Blue Page
directory."
"Mr. Blue Page, this is Jan
Fredrico. My daughter has a cold
and my kidneys have a slight ache. I
would like for you to give me the
names of the nutrients that specialize
in the areas of our illness."

Insight On Trumpism And The Only Thing That Can Save USA From Total Doom

"Very well, madam. In the area
of the   kidneys, the association of
VC and Cranberry handle that, and
in the area of colds and flu, the
association of Garlic, Echinacea, and
Golden Seal handle that. Will that be
all, madam?"

"Yes sir, and thank you very
much," said Jan. Taking advantage
of their-walk in policy, Jan didn't have
to wait long before she was able to
see VC, the very powerful vitamin C
antioxidant.

"Mrs. Fredrico," said VC, " We
give our doses in mostly tablet form.
I am of the water soluble type, the
body does not store my doses.
Taking too much of my dose is
washed out with the urine. But,
taking too much of my dose also may
cause diarrhea or stomach soreness
in some humans.

Rule number one for dealing with
your kidney problem is to keep
drinking lots of water, then take 2000
mg. of vitamin C tablets three or four
times a day after a meal, also take
2000 mg. of cranberry fruit capsules
three of four times a day after a meal.
That should take care of your
problem, Mrs. Fredrico."

Jan next proceeded to take her
daughter by the association of Garlic,
Echinacea, and Golden Seal to take
care of her cold. After a short wait
Jan and her daughter were lead in to

Insight On Trumpism And The Only Thing That Can Save USA From Total Doom

see Hannah-Garlic.

Hannah-Garlic came from one of
the most powerful and popular of all
herb families. Even   the Roman
army would not go into battle without
a member of the garlic family coming
along.

Hannah-Garlic instructed Jan to
give Melinda throat lozenges if
needed, then give her a dose of about
1400 mg. of odor controlled garlic,
three or four times a day after a meal,
also give her a 1500 mg. dose of
combination echinacea-golden seal
three or four times a day after a meal.

"You should see some obvious
improvement in twenty four hours; if
not take the super MD highway to the
cure all metropolis.

"It is also helpful to take heavy
doses of vitamin C after a meal at the
beginning of a cold. But, only at the
beginning of a cold, because if
congestion sets in, vitamin C tends
to make it worse. Warning: Never
take vitamin C or others nutrients on
an empty stomach," she said.
After thoroughly going over
everything, Hannah-Garlic said, "
That is it, Mrs. Fredrico, do you
understand all of my instructions?"

"Yes, Herb Garlic and thank you
very much." While driving home Jan
reminded herself to do her neck
exercises when she got home. It has

Insight On Trumpism And The Only Thing That Can Save USA From Total Doom

been quite awhile since stress has
caused her neck to tense up, but she
Decided that she would go ahead
and do the exercises anyway.

Jan believed that feeling stress is
a normal part of life. The better one
learns how to deal with life's
frustrations the better one will be able
to cope with stress. Stress affects
people in many different ways. It
may affect some in physical ways
such as headaches, neck aches,
shoulder aches, etc.

To deal with physical aches it is
helpful to do these exercises. These
exercises are done sitting on the side
of the bed. Sit on the side of the bed
with feet apart flat on the floor for
balance. With both hands rolled into
a fist, place them thumbs inward
down on the bed several inches from
the body on each side.

Start the first exercise by twisting
the neck and entire upper body
counter-clockwise as far as possible,
then twist the neck and entire upper
body clockwise as far as possible.
Do these exercises in sets of one
hundred as many times as one
desires.

Start the second exercise by
leaning the head as far as possible on
the right shoulder, then lean the head
as far as possible on the left
shoulder. Do these exercises in sets
of one hundred as many times as one

desires.

Start the third exercise by
leaning the chin as far as possible
down on the chest, then lift the head
backward as far as possible. Do
these exercises in sets of one
hundred as many times as one
desires.

Chapter 5
On the morning of the big town
hall meeting, Jim-Niacin followed his
daily routine of taking care of the
citizens of Health-land Kingdom. Jim-
Niacin tried to take care of all loose
ends concerning the town hall
meeting by making a lot of last minute
phone calls. He rehearsed the
program with his cousin B-12 who
would be the moderator for tonight's
town hall meeting.

At seven o'clock p.m. sharp Jim-
Niacin arrived at the local high school
gymnasium, the location of tonight's
town hall meeting. The meeting was
scheduled to start at eight o'clock
p.m. There were several satellite
trucks already in place when he
arrived. There were the local radio
and TV crews as well as reporters
from the big super cure all metropolis.

Arriving at the high school was
familiar territory for Captain Fredrico.
He had walked at the high school
track three or more times a week for
several years. The high school track

Insight On Trumpism And The Only Thing That Can Save USA From Total Doom

was a popular walking place for the citizens of Health-land Kingdom. Captain Fredrico felt that walking or some type of physical fitness program is a must to maintain good health.

It is a fact that one in good physical condition has almost a ten times better chance of surviving a heart attack, stroke, or any ailment. Also, physical activity plays a big role in controlling diabetes. A big help with diabetes is controlling what one eats. Most humans can control diabetes by cutting way back on starches and sweets and taking a chromium picolinate at each meal.

One needs to eat less meat and include more peas, beans, fresh fruits, and raw vegetables. One needs to include at least one raw fruit or vegetable at each meal because cooking and microwaving food destroys all enzymes and most vitamins.

Enzymes are involved in almost every bodily function, especially the digestive process. Enzymes are mostly divided into two groups: digestive enzymes and metabolic enzymes. The digestive enzymes break down food enabling the body to function properly.

The human body manufactures a limited supply of enzymes, but in order to prevent indigestion and other digestive problems one should get as

Insight On Trumpism And The Only Thing That Can Save USA From Total Doom

many enzymes as possible from raw
food. Otherwise, the body's limited
supply becomes depleted.

Jim could see that there was
going to be a very big turnout for
tonight's event. It seemed like his
hard work on getting the word out had
paid off. Several tables were set up
at one end of the gymnasium to try
to accommodate as many as possible
on the big panel of vitamins, minerals,
humans, herbs, and other nutrients.

Everyone were handed a
program as they filed into the
gymnasium. It read that, "We will not
be able to accommodate everyone
due to the time it would take. The
moderator will ask all questions, but
he will take a few written questions
from the audience." At exactly eight
p.m. sharp B-12 (vitamin B-12)
strode up to the podium.

"Greetings, my fellow vitamins,
minerals, humans, herbs, and other
nutrients, I'm B-12 your moderator for
tonight's town hall meeting," he said.
"First I would like to welcome our
town's fathers, celebrities, and all
other dignitaries to this town hall
meeting. Now, I would like to thank
the vitamin that made it all happen.
He is truly another unsung hero.
Many of you here tonight probably
have never heard of him, but all of
the while he has been out there
everyday doing his job. He is one of
the lesser known members of the

Insight On Trumpism And The Only Thing That Can Save USA From Total Doom

powerful B vitamin family. I am proud
to say this truly unsung hero is my
first cousin Jim-Niacin (vitamin B-3).
Stand up, Jim."

"Thank you, thank you, thank
you," said Jim-Niacin as he stood and
the audience loudly applauded.
"Now," said B-12, "before we get
into questions and answers we are
going to let several members on our
panel down here give their name and
vocation. We will start with me. I'm
B-12 (vitamin B-12). One of my
many jobs is to assure proper
digestion and the absorption of food."

"I'm Jane-Ginkgo Biloba. I'm a
very well known herb. I'm mostly
Known for improving memory."
"I'm Sammy-Oat Bran Tablets.
I'm known for my fiber. Fiber does so
many things, for now I will mention
just two, I lower the blood cholesterol
and help stabilize blood sugar."

"I'm Eddie-calcium. I'm a mineral
and I do many things. I'm most
needed for strong bones and teeth
and to help lower blood pressure."
"I'm Mary-Magnesium. I'm a
mineral and of the many things that I
do, enzyme activity is most vital. I
also assist calcium and potassium
uptake."

"I'm Sue-Chromium. I'm a
mineral and of the many things that I
do, maintaining stable blood sugar
levels is most vital."

Insight On Trumpism And The Only Thing That Can Save USA From Total Doom

"I'm VA (vitamin A). I'm a
vitamin and lesser known antioxidant.
My main job is protecting the eyes
and some skin problems."
"I'm Dee Dee (vitamin D). I'm a
vitamin, and I'm needed for the
absorption   of calcium and
phosphorus."

"I'm Ned-Zinc. I'm a mineral and
of the many things that I do, keeping
the prostate gland healthy is most
vital."

"I'm Kenny-Saw Pametto. I'm an
herb, my main job is to prevent the
enlargement of the prostate gland."
"I'm Gina-Evening Primrose Oil.
I'm an essential fatty acid. I'm a
necessity that cannot be made by
the human body. I do many things,
but improving the skin is my favorite."

"I'm Patty-Potassium. I'm a
mineral. Of my many jobs I will
name just a few. I help maintain a
healthy nervous system and regulate
heart rhythm, also I help control the
body's water balance."

"I'm Hannah-Garlic. I'm an herb.
I detoxify and protect the body
against infections. I help lower blood
pressure, aid circulation and perform
many other functions."

"I'm Henry-Acidophilus. I'm a
friendly bacteria. My main job is to
aid digestion."

Insight On Trumpism And The Only Thing That Can Save USA From Total Doom

"I'm Bonnie-Papaya. I'm an
herb. I aid digestion. I'm good for
heartburn, indigestion, and bowel
disorders."

"I'm Brad-Cranberry Fruit. I'm an
herb. I'm helpful for fighting infections
of the urinary track."

"I'm Stewart-Ginger Root. I'm an
herb. I do many things, but cleaning
the colon, reducing spasms, and
stomach cramps is my favorite."

"I'm Calvin-Fenugreek. I'm good
for the stomach, intestines, eyes,
asthma, sinus, inflammation, and lung
disorders. I also increase sexual
desire."

"I'm Edna-Echinacea. I'm an
herb. I have anti viral properties
and I help boost the immune system.
I'm very helpful against colds and flu."
"I'm Gene-Golden Seal. I'm an
herb. I act as an antibiotic, and have
anti-inflammatory and antibacterial
properties."

I'm David-Dandelion root. I am
an herb. I help cleanse the blood
stream and liver and increase the
production of bile. I'm used as a
diuretic. I help reduce uric acid and
improve functioning of the stomach
and other vital organs.

"That is the last introduction we
will have time for," said B-12. "Now, I
will ask the panel a few written

Insight On Trumpism And The Only Thing That Can Save USA From Total Doom

questions given to me from the audience, but first let me explain our role here. Number one is we try to be the first line of defense on protecting Health-land Kingdom from Mr. Disease and his cohorts.

"We have some citizens who don't believe in us and won't use our services. The next thing is we don't try to be everything to everybody, our services and abilities are limited.

We encourage anyone that has doubts or don't believe in us to take the super MD highway to the cure all metropolis. Still, there is a lot we can do to keep Mr. Disease and his friends from gaining a foothold here in Health-land Kingdom.

"Very important: When taking the super MD highway to the cure all metropolis, make sure you tell them which of our services you are maintaining.

"Now, when I ask a question to the panel, please let those that specialize in that particular area of expertise answer the question. Time will not allow me to ask but only a few questions. My first question to the panel is what can we do to   combat prostate disease?" he asked.
"I'm Ned-Zinc, and I recommend 50 mg. of zinc per day."

"I'm Larry-Pumpkin Seed Oil, and I recommend 1000 mg. of pumpkin

seed oil per day."
"I'm Kenny-Saw Pametto, and I
recommend 160 mg. of saw pametto
extract twice per day."
"I'm VE (vitamin E), and I
recommend 1000 I.U. of vitamin E
per day."
"I'm Jim-Niacin, and I
recommend my maintenance dose of
250 mg. of niacin per day."
"Is there anyone else?" said B-
12. "So, that gives us five weapons
to fight prostate disease, and I'm
pretty darn sure that anyone that
arms themselves with these weapons
will be able to keep Mr. prostate
disease away for a very long time, if
not forever. My next question to the
panel is what can we do to deal with
diabetes disease?"

"I'm Sue-Chromium, and I
recommend 200 mg. of chromium
picolinate three times a day at meal
time. I also would like to elaborate a
little on this terrible disease.

"Diet plays a   major role in
controlling this terrible disease.
Everyone with this disease should be
able to home check his blood sugar
level and keep it under control. But,
controlling blood sugar is not the only
problem diabetics face.

"There are problems with the
eyes, blood circulation, and many
others. There is a problem with nerve
damage (neuropathy) especially in
the lower extremities," she concluded.

Insight On Trumpism And The Only Thing That Can Save USA From Total Doom

"I'm VE (vitamin E), and I recommend 1000 I.U. of vitamin E per day. Being a natural blood thinner makes me a great asset to a diabetic."

"I'm Jim-Niacin, and I recommend my maintenance dose of 250 mg. of niacin once per day for one not showing any diabetic symptoms. On the other hand, for anyone experiencing the symptoms of diabetes, especially numbness in the lower extremities I recommend my unclogging dose of 250 mg. of niacin twice per day.

"Too high of a dose of niacin can cause liver damage and high blood sugar levels, but too low of a dose does no good. The 500 mg. maximum dose per day seems to be just enough to be effective.

"There have been many lower extremities cut off because of diabetes, but I truly believe that if they had only given Jim-Niacin a chance I would have saved some of those limbs."

"Is there anyone else?" said B-12. "There it is folks, three powerful weapons to deal with this scourge diabetes. Now, for the final question of the evening, the question is what can we do to prevent extremely dry skin?"

Insight On Trumpism And The Only Thing That Can Save USA From Total Doom

"I'm Gina-Evening Primrose Oil, I'm an essential fatty acid and I'm one of the good oils that the body needs for beautiful skin. I recommend 1000-3000 mg. of evening primrose oil per day."

"I'm Jim-Niacin. In my view problems with dry skin, toe nail funguses, dandruff, and other skin problems is almost always a problem with blood circulation especially in the capillaries and small blood vessels.

"For extremely dry skin I recommend my unclogging dose of 250 mg. twice per day after a meal until the extremely dry skin condition has been cured, then throttle down to 250 mg. once a day for maintenance. But, be aware, most humans fear me, and for good reason, because my doses are no Sunday picnic or stroll through the park. My doses may heat up your skin like it is on fire and turn it as red as a beet.

"This flushing process is unpredictable, sometimes it will not happen at all, then other times it will last anywhere from five minutes to thirty minutes. It may not be pleasant, but it is my only way of unclogging the capillaries and small blood vessels," said Jim-Niacin.

"Is there anyone else?" said B-12. "What more could one ask for; those were two of the most powerful remedies that I ever heard of in

Insight On Trumpism And The Only Thing That Can Save USA From Total Doom

dealing with a pesky humiliating dry skin condition.

"Remember, a dry skin problem is not something to be taken lightly, because you can see what is happening to the outer skin, but what's taking place inside with the vital organs could be a lot worse. "Citizens of Health-land Kingdom, that will end our town hall meeting for tonight, I would like to thank everyone for coming. Have a safe drive home," he said.

Chapter 6

Captain Fredrico was very impressed with the town hall meeting, especially learning how to deal with his long time dry skin problem and toe nail fungus. It had got to the point that he hated to take a shower.

It was bad enough struggling through the warmer months of the year, but the approach of winter was almost terrifying because a dry skin problem becomes much worse during the winter months. Much of the time during the winter he had to resort to what is called a bird bath by washing only his arm pits and private area. He had tried all kinds of oils, both internal and external. He had traveled on the super MD highway to the cure all metropolis, but all to no avail. Since the town hall meeting he had started off on Jim-Niacin's unclogging dose of 250 mg. of niacin

Insight On Trumpism And The Only Thing That Can Save USA From Total Doom

twice a day after a meal.

The resulting benefits were
obvious within a couple of days.
Within days the treatment was so
effective that the captain could barely
wait to jump into the shower for the
slightest reason. Also, within days
his toe nails had started clearing and
should be completely clear within a
few months.

Also, in a few months the
mayoral election will be taking place.
Captain Fredrico felt very good about
his chances   of winning. According
to the latest poll he had a four point
lead.

That night as he and Jan were
setting in the den watching TV,
Captain Fredrico said, "You know,
Jan, if I do become mayor of Health-
land Kingdom I'm going to recognize
Jim-Niacin by declaring a Jim-Niacin
day."

"I know, dear, how much you
love Jim-Niacin. He made it possible
for you to be able to take regular
showers again without you having to
lotion down almost your whole body."
"I don't care how much he is
feared and misunderstood," said the
Captain. "As far as I'm concerned
Jim-Niacin is a miracle vitamin."

"I agree, my darling husband,
about Jim-Niacin's abilities, if humans
would just give him a chance he

Insight On Trumpism And The Only Thing That Can Save USA From Total Doom

would save most of the lower
extremities that are being lost
because of Mr. Diabetes Disease."

The Captain got up from his
recliner, walked over to Jan and gave
her a warm tender kiss on her waiting
luscious lips and said, "I'm off to bed,
dear, I'll wait up for you."
"I won't be long, dear," said Jan.

Things had been rather calm in
Health-land Kingdom for the last few
months VC, VE, and John-pyridoxine
all were very busy taking care of the
town's population. About the only
thing going on was the mayoral
election coming up very soon.

They all thought the town hall
meeting did a lot of good for the
community. They felt it educated the
citizens that there was a lot they
could do for themselves concerning
their health care.

That means that one will not
have   to jump on the super MD
highway for the slightest little pin prick
or minor inconvenience. Sure, there
is only so much we vitamins,
minerals, herbs, etc. can do to
promote health, we don't try to be
everything to everybody.
After the town hall meeting Mr.

Insight On Trumpism And The Only Thing That Can Save USA From Total Doom

Disease was steaming mad. He was even thinking of
calling a meeting of all the different diseases. The
nerve
of those vitamins, minerals, humans,
herbs and other nutrients trying to get
together and put him and his friends
out of business.

They want to try to put his most
successful friends like cancer,
diabetes, heart disease, and AIDS
out of business. He was not having
it; that was not going to be tolerated.
Mr. Disease started planning.

He would try to attack their left flank
by bringing back some of his old
friends like the Black Plague,
Tuberculosis, and West Nile, next he
would try to rush their right flank with
AIDS to try to split their force, then he
would try to rout them up the middle
with lots of Cancer and Heart
Disease.

I will take no prisoners. Who do
they think this is, this is Mr. Disease
and I don't play, I even quit school
because they had recess. It is on.
How dare they have this town hall
meeting to try and get rid of me and
my friends.

After a long hot summer the day
of the mayoral election had finally
arrived and it looked like it was going
to be a big turn out. At seven o'clock
p.m. Captain Fredrico, Jan, Bob, and
Melinda had comfortable seats at

Insight On Trumpism And The Only Thing That Can Save USA From Total Doom

election headquarters. All of the
election precincts closed at seven
o'clock p.m. sharp.

The captain and his family
started   watching the tally on the
big electronic board as the precincts
came in. Captain Fredrico jumped
out to an early four point lead and
was able to maintain the lead
throughout the night as the precincts
came in. Then, finally the election
supervisor announced, "Citizens of
Health-land Kingdom the mayor elect
is Orry Fredrico." Within seconds
several microphones were thrust in
Captain Fredrico's face.

A reporter was almost yelling,
"Captain Fredrico, how does it feel
being the mayor elect of Health-land
Kingdom."

"First, I would like to thank my
family and all of the volunteers that
worked so hard on my behalf to make
this   happen. Next, I would like to
thank all of the citizens of Health-land
Kingdom who had the faith and trust
in me and backed it up by turning out
to vote for me.

"Also, I would like to inform those
that did not vote for me that I will be
mayor of all the citizens of Health-
land Kingdom. Finally, I would like to
thank my opponent for a good clean
hard fought campaign. Thanks again
everyone. Good night."

Insight On Trumpism And The Only Thing That Can Save USA From Total Doom

Chapter 7

About one month after Captain Fredrico had been sworn in as mayor of Health-land Kingdom, he announced that the first Saturday in March would be recognized by the town as Jim-Niacin's day.

On the morning of the first Saturday in March Mayor Fredrico stood at the podium at Healthy living park before a very large crowd.

"Citizens of Health-land Kingdom, today as your mayor I am proclaiming today as Jim-Niacin's day. We have on hand plenty of free food, drinks, and entertainment. To kick off this festive day, I'm going to deliver this short speech about the vitamin citizen we are celebrating today.

"Citizens of Health-land, Jim-Niacin is sort of an enigma. Many here had never heard of him, and of those that had, many of them fear and hate him. Still there is a great many that love this vitamin to death.

"I myself am one of those that dearly love Jim-Niacin and the good work he does. I am not telling you what I heard about Jim-Niacin, I'm telling you what I've personally experienced with my dealing with Jim-Niacin. I'm giving it to you first hand, straight from the horse's mouth.

Insight On Trumpism And The Only Thing That Can Save USA From Total Doom

"As I've told my wife and many
others, I don't care what anyone
says, to me Jim-Niacin is a miracle
vitamin. This small, quiet, lowly
member of the powerful B vitamin
family is a Godsend as far as I'm
concerned. As a proud virile human
male I think of the many, many years
that I suffered with extremely dry
skin.

"For years I tried everything to
get relief from this annoying dry skin
condition. Even at the cure all
metropolis they just prescribed an
extremely expensive body cream that
did little better than cheap over-the-
counter lotions.

"Bathing and warm water had
become the enemy. Washing only
arm pits and the private area was
becoming the norm, and I just hated
my predicament. To me cleanliness
is next to   Godliness.

"Sure, I had heard of Jim-Niacin,
but it was mainly bad stuff, I never
knew about his real power until I
attended the town hall meeting. Over
the years the dry skin problem was
getting worse. Some type of fungus
had invaded my toe nails and my skin
was losing its luster in a few
locations.

"The battle for healthy skin was a
battle I knew I was losing , but no one
could help me and I didn't know what

Insight On Trumpism And The Only Thing That Can Save USA From Total Doom

to do. All of my life I've never been a
quitter, I knew there was an answer,
the problem was finding it, so I just
kept on searching and searching.

"I was at my wits end, nothing or
no one seemed able to help me find
relief from my extremely dry skin
condition. Then, at the final hour
when all seemed lost and there was
no hope left, Jim-Niacin came riding
in on a big white horse at the town
hall meeting.

"At the town hall meeting Jim-
Niacin gave out his unclogging dose
of 250 mg. twice a day after a meal.
The first thing is I must warn you that
taking Jim-Niacin's unclogging dose is
no cake walk or stroll through the
park. That is the reason many who
have tried taking Jim's doses don't
like him and is afraid of him.

"When Jim goes to work
unclogging those capillaries and small
blood vessels it is not pleasant by any
means. This flushing process varies
in intensity, sometimes it may be
mild, then at other times your skin
may feel like it is literally on fire.

"This flushing process may last
anywhere from five to thirty minutes,
but seldom lasts more than thirty
minutes. I have no evidence to
support this, but I believe diabetes
itself is caused by a deficiency in
niacin, chromium, and a few other
nutrients.

Insight On Trumpism And The Only Thing That Can Save USA From Total Doom

"Citizens of Health-land I could
go on and on praising Jim-Niacin
because in the past he truly has been
an unsung hero. I will add this and
come to a close. Don't ever go over
his maximum 500 mg. daily dose or it
could cause liver damage.

"In closing, I will assure you that
his unclogging dose got rid of my
dandruff, dry skin, toe nail fungus,
etc. Stand up Jim-Niacin and say a
few words," concluded Captain
Fredrico.

As Jim-Niacin arrived at the
podium he stood tall and proud.
The audience went wild with
applause, then chanted, "We love you
Jim, we love you Jim, we love you
"Thank you, thank you, thank
you," said Jim-Niacin, "and may God
bless this great town and keep it
healthy always."

THE END

**ENJOY BOLD RAW UNCUT CREATIVE WRITING BY
SELF-MADE WRITER FREDDIE L SIRMANS SR.**

**PURCHASE OR READ EXCERPTS BY VISITING HIS
WEBSITE AT:
www.FLSirmans.com**